MIDCENTURY
CHRISTMAS

by SARAH ARCHER

STOCKING STUFFER *edition*

THE COUNTRYMAN PRESS
A DIVISION OF W. W. NORTON & COMPANY
Independent Publishers Since 1923

FOR MY MOTHER, WHO HAS THE SAME HANDWRITING AS SANTA CLAUS

For information about permission to reproduce selections from this book,
write to Permissions, The Countryman Press, 500 Fifth Avenue, New York, NY 10110

For information about special discounts for bulk purchases, please contact
W. W. Norton Special Sales at specialsales@wwnorton.com or 800-233-4830

Manufacturing by RR Donnelley, Shenzhen
Book design by LeAnna Weller Smith
Production manager: Devon Zahn

The Countryman Press
www.countrymanpress.com

A division of W. W. Norton & Company, Inc.
500 Fifth Avenue, New York, NY 10110
www.wwnorton.com

978-1-68268-336-1

10 9 8 7 6 5 4 3 2 1

CONTENTS

INTRODUCTION

Christmas has a way of making us wistful for the past. Even when I was a kid, longing for an orange-and-black Garfield telephone during the gadget-obsessed 1980s, Santa Claus himself was pretty low tech. He may have brought us newfangled toys, but his accoutrements never seemed to change: the sleigh, the red suit, and the handwritten thank-you notes left near the tableau of cookies and carrots we'd put out for him and his eight reindeer on December 24.

House Beautiful, December 1963.

That's why I was intrigued a few years ago when I stumbled upon an article about Soviet-era New Year's cards that depicted Santa Claus's Cold War counterpart, Grandfather Frost, riding rocket ships and delivering presents from low orbit. With a little digging, I discovered that our own Santa Claus had dabbled in space travel, too. There are traces of it evident today: NORAD still "tracks" Santa on radar, as it has since 1955. The period from 1945 to 1970 took Christmas in America (and, indeed, New Year's celebrations in the USSR) on a sharp detour away from the Victorian charm of the Christmases that so many of us remember—even those of us who grew up at the end of the Cold War, or right after it. It's an exercise in futuristic nostalgia, like watching a sci-fi series from the '60s.

Cover, *Weather Bureau Topics*, December 1958.

New Year's card from the USSR, 1960s.

Fueled by a sense of optimism and widespread prosperity, postwar Americans embraced a high-tech version of a holiday that had long been steeped in ancient lore and symbols of an old-fashioned way of life: sleighs, candles, handmade toys, and the worship of trees. In the mid-1960s, a crackling Yule log glowed from Zenith television sets, and Christmas trees fashioned from shiny aluminum sparkled in the winter light. Taken together, the enthusiasm for new materials, science, space travel, bold graphics, and a special love of convenience foods paint a picture of a society that was exhilarated by the possibilities of its new superpower status and a bit tentative, even frightened, of the postwar world it now occupied. The material culture and popular entertainment of the era put a brave face on it all, but the mysteries of space exploration, atomic energy, and the prospect of armed conflicts with the Soviet Union were very frightening to contemplate. This curious mixture of economic security and global anxiety made Americans want to nest like never before—the most extreme iteration of this impulse was the iconic home bomb shelter stocked with board games and canned goods.

American Christmas
Card, ca. 1930s.

In every era, the celebration of Christmas elicits a sense of wonder and childlike glee in adults and children alike. Each holiday season, the Christmas story reminds us that our own families and circles of friends are their own sorts of miracles to be celebrated. We cultivate a sense of magic around the holiday to remind ourselves of our good fortune, or to make manifest our hopes for better times to come. In the postwar era, a spacefaring Santa, ultramodern Christmas cards and wrapping paper, aluminum trees, and an array of scientifically and domestically inspired toys gave tentatively optimistic Americans a way to make the Space Age their own, even familiar and cozy; something to behold in awe, not something to fear.

OPPOSITE LEFT: Cover of the Dell *Santa Claus Funnies*, December 1959, Western Printing & Litho Company.

OPPOSITE RIGHT: An American Christmas card, 1950s.

ABOVE: An illuminated Santa figurine, Paramount, 1950s–60s.

In 1957, Theodor Geisel, better known as Dr. Seuss, •
introduced American readers to their very own
Atomic Age Scrooge: the Grinch, a sinister green
critter who hated Christmas so much he vowed to
"steal" it from the cheery citizens of Whoville, as
though Christmas itself were a commodity for sale
at a department store. Geisel's beloved holiday tale,
which has since been adapted for television, film,
and Broadway, was intended as a good-natured
but serious critique of postwar America's love affair
with all the commercial trappings of the holiday
season. The inspiring moral of *How the Grinch
Stole Christmas!* is that Christmas isn't a thing to be
stolen at all, but a celebration of family and good
cheer that arrives on cue every December, presents
or no presents.

Theodore Geisel, American writer and cartoonist,
at work on *How the Grinch Stole Christmas!*, 1957.

"Marley's ghost appearing to Scrooge."
Illustration by S. J. Woolf, *Century*
magazine, 1911.

Charles Dickens's 1843 holiday masterpiece, *A Christmas Carol*, gave us the ultimate Christmas antihero, Ebenezer Scrooge. A cruel taskmaster, Scrooge is ungenerous to his sympathetic employee, Bob Cratchit, and his family. When Scrooge sees the light on Christmas morning after he's visited by the ghosts of Christmas Past, Present, and Future, he responds by sharing his material abundance with strangers and colleagues alike: gifts for the Cratchit children, a Christmas turkey, and a long-overdue raise for Bob. It's a happy ending that made perfect sense in Dickens's time, when unregulated child labor and urban poverty were pressing issues in Great Britain. Scrooge's Christmas enlightenment underscores the idea—relatively new at the time—that material prosperity should be shared by everyone.

How the Grinch Stole Christmas!, based on the book by Dr. Seuss, directed by Chuck Jones and Ben Washam, 1966.

The Grinch's tale wraps up very differently: in a climate of planned obsolescence, new shopping malls, mail-order catalogs, department-store Santas, and television programming designed around commercials, Geisel's message to American readers was that none of us really need presents—a new dishwasher, a new car, or any of the glittering decorations that signal the arrival of Christmas each December. Geisel's book was wildly popular, but his message was only partially received. During the postwar era, Americans shopped, decorated, and feasted like never before, making new, formerly exotic materials and technologies an integral part of this well-loved holiday. By the 1950s, more Americans than ever before could consider themselves middle class, and novel materials like plastic and aluminum made the look and feel of Christmas decidedly modern. By the 1960s, a typical Christmas tableau in a department store window might look more like the Jetsons than the Cratchits.

Entertaining Gifts

fun to give or receive—a delight for all a

Color TV brings amazingly vi
life-like programs. See big r
tangular picture sizes, eas
than-ever color tuning.

Clock Radio lulls and wakes you to music, provides day-long pleasure as well.

Console Stereo adds dimension to records and radio, style to your home. Some have built-in tape recorder.

2

The period that immediately followed the end of World War II transformed the United States socially, economically, politically, and visually. Not only did it feel different, everything looked different, too. Part of this was the change in the physical landscape, which blossomed with new subdivisions and tract houses, but it was also thanks to the new look of postwar modernism coupled with the aesthetics of the Space Age. After the war, with industrial productivity at an all-time high, American consumers could afford gifts and decorations on a much larger scale; the customs of the well-to-do could now belong to almost everyone. The economist John Kenneth Galbraith wrote in 1958 that "the ordinary individual has access to amenities—foods, entertainment, personal transportation, and plumbing—in which not even the rich rejoiced a century ago."

"Treasury of Christmas Ideas," Western Light and Telephone Company Home Services Department, 1960s.

Since the mid-nineteenth century, the celebration of Christmas in America had been an exercise in nostalgia, during which people living in a time of rapid industrialization and social change cultivated rituals that evoked an imagined, preindustrial past. But the Christmas season historically has also been a time for trying things on and switching things up, and reveling in the novelty of a topsy-turvy world. Once World War II was over, Americans developed a holiday culture that turned the old Victorian status quo upside down, and made a Christmas wish for something new: the future.

"Treasury of Christmas Ideas," Western Light and Telephone
Company Home Services Department, 1960s.

HOLIDA

TREASURY
OF
CHRISTMAS
IDEAS

THINGS TO MAKE   **LIGHT-TIME DECORATING**   **GIFT IDEAS**

ALL IS BRIGHT: DECORATING

The days and weeks that lead up to Christmas are almost as much fun as the day itself—even more fun, in a sense, because they're bursting with anticipation. The rituals of decorating and baking help distract us.

Barbara Stanwyck and Dennis Morgan in the film *Christmas in Connecticut*, directed by Peter Godfrey, Warner Bros., 1945.

Many of my favorite Christmas memories are actually of the lead-up, rather than the day itself: bringing out boxes of ornaments, unwrapping the Nativity set, opening new packages of tinsel (only to find pieces of it months later hiding in crevices all over the living room). Learning the tricks of the trade as a child, like how to string Christmas tree lights, or the right way to bake gingerbread, makes one feel skilled in a culturally specific way, like part of the tribe. And no matter the style of one's holiday tableau, we have the postwar era to thank for many of these rituals and the material conveniences that make the month-long marathon of decor and entertaining more streamlined; after all, spending cozy time at home was at the center of midcentury life.

House Beautiful, December 1961.

Postwar homeowners found themselves living in a new kind of America. In 1940, 43.6 percent of Americans owned their home. By 1960, 61.9 percent did. This was due in large measure to the benefits of the Servicemen's Readjustment Act of 1944, better known as the G.I. Bill, which gave returning soldiers funding to start new businesses, attend college or graduate school, and obtain home mortgages. In 1947, developer William Levitt built the first of many "Levittowns" on 4,000 acres of Long Island farmland. Across the country, home building in new suburbs proliferated. In 1944, 114,000 new homes were built, and in 1950, that figure was 1.7 million.

The focus on home and hearth was not new during the postwar era; the nineteenth century gave rise to what historians call the "cult of domesticity," as industrialization increasingly split the roles of men and women between the outside world of business and commerce and the interior world of family, housework, and nurturance. But Americans did have a good new reason to fixate on the domestic front. With Great Britain ravaged by the war even in victory, the two new superpowers that emerged in 1945—the United States and the Soviet Union—were both large, formidable, and ideologically opposed to one another.

Newfound prosperity coupled with worry about possible conflict with the Soviets meant that middle-class homeowners doubled down on domesticity. Their increased buying power drove sales of home appliances and improvements to rates far higher than the consumption of other goods like clothing, travel, or entertainment. In 1958, Bank of America unveiled the first consumer credit card, and by 1960 there were more than 100 million of them in use in the United States. Pundits characterized Communism as a threat not just to the American way of life in general, but to the American family unit in particular; the ideology of shared resources undercut the nesting instinct of American parents to provide for their kids and build a secure, happy home. Faced with the prospect of a frightening global conflict waged across the Iron Curtain, coziness wasn't just comforting, it was patriotic. In 1948, before his name became synonymous with suburban tract houses, William Levitt summarized it perfectly: "No man who owns his own house and lot can be a Communist. He has too much to do."

House Beautiful,
December 1954.

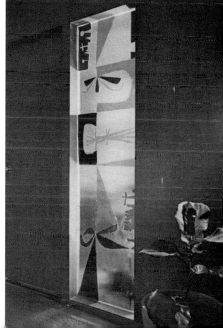

Beautiful, December 1954.

The 1950s introduced new technology to the world, and with it a whole new visual vocabulary, much of it derived from efforts by designers and illustrators to make complex scientific ideas clear to a wide range of people. Postwar America was living through the age of the atom, and the 1950s and '60s became known as the Atomic Age because the end of World War II made nuclear energy part of a national conversation. Like electricity before it, the awesome power of nuclear energy was communicated to a wide audience through the design of objects, graphics, and animation. A 1956 book by German physicist Dr. Heinz Haber, *Our Friend the Atom*, and its companion episode of the TV series *Disneyland*, painted a serious but optimistic picture of atomic energy for young viewers by interpreting its power through a modern retelling of "The Fisherman and the Genie," one of the stories told by Scheherazade in *One Thousand and One Nights*. Atomic power is the proverbial "genie in the bottle," and the "three wishes" are the (rather idealized) benefits that nuclear energy can offer mankind: power, food and health, and peace.

Walt Disney consults with Dr. Heinz Haber during the making of *Our Friend the Atom*. California, ca. 1957.

The stylized model of the atom comprised of three or four ovals through which one or more dots appear to "orbit" became visual shorthand for both nuclear power itself and a more general kind of scientific progress that seemed zippy and exciting. Atoms were in the zeitgeist in the 1950s and '60s, appearing in toys and comic books, in the design of lighting fixtures and tableware. This design perfectly complemented the forms and aesthetics of modernism, the early twentieth-century movement that eschewed ornament and embraced abstraction, basic forms, and bold color.

Atomic missile pedal car,
Murray Ohio Manufacturing Company, 1958.

To imagine the architectural style sometimes referred to as the Googie movement, named for a now-defunct California coffee shop designed by architect John Lautner in 1949, picture neon-lit road signs with zigzag or starburst details, or a hamburger stand with a big sweeping roof shaped like a parabola. Googie landmarks include Betty Willis's iconic 1959 "Welcome to Fabulous Las Vegas" sign, Edward E. Carlson and John Graham Jr.'s Space Needle in Seattle, and Eero Saarinen's TWA Flight Center in New York City. The Space Needle and the TWA Flight Center were both built in 1962. The Jetsons' cartoon space-home also could be characterized as Googie design. The stylized Atomic Age imagery that evoked speed, movement, and light was also inherently festive, and it was quickly adopted by the designers of Christmas cards, wrapping paper, and toys, giving midcentury Christmas celebrations a brand new look. Even the old-fashioned Christmas tree and its sparkling glass ornaments were suddenly cutting edge. The humble Christmas ball might just be the perfect postwar holiday object: round, conical, or teardrop-shaped, brightly colored, abstract, and light as a feather. These Christmas ornaments somehow anticipated the aesthetics of the Atomic Age by at least a century.

"It's Christmas Again,"
print advertisement
for The Airlines of the
United States, 1945.

Three glass Christmas ornaments manufactured by Corning Glass Works, ca. 1940s–60s.

Ornaments

The origin of the Christmas ball can be traced to Germany, which was the global capital of Christmas production in the nineteenth and early twentieth century. Evergreen Christmas trees had long been decorated in Germany and elsewhere in Northern Europe with edible treats like pastries, candy, and apples—all symbols of festive abundance to be enjoyed during the coldest months. Though it can't be proven beyond doubt, it seems likely that the idea of a shiny glass "apple" to decorate Christmas trees symbolized the spirit of the season: a piece of fruit that would never go bad glimmering from a tree that would never turn brown.

KING SIZE

10¢ 10¢

75

ORNAMENT
HANGERS

FOR LONG NEEDLE TREES

Ornament hangers, 1950s.

F. W. Woolworth began selling German Christmas ornaments in the 1890s, and Woolworth's stores were soon selling about $25 million worth of ornaments each year. World War I temporarily halted the import of German goods to the United States, but production and sales resumed throughout the 1920s and '30s. Another enterprising importer, however, sensed that with another war increasingly likely, bigger changes were afoot in the global economy. Max Eckardt, a native of Germany, had been successfully importing hand-painted glass Christmas ornaments from Bavaria since the 1920s, working out of a warehouse on the Harlem River in New York City. Selling them under the names Shiny Brite and Max Eckardt & Sons, Eckardt had relatives and employees in Germany silvering and decorating the ornaments by hand, applying glitter and color to figures of Santa Claus and his elves, lanterns, stars, and cozy cottages.

Assorted Shiny Brite ornaments from the 1960s, shown in a vintage Shiny Brite box from the same period.

The mechanics of mass production favored a simpler shape, however, bringing the spherical Christmas bauble back into vogue. In 1937, Eckardt and a representative from F. W. Woolworth contacted the New York–based Corning Glass Works to see if they could produce ornaments in the United States. Corning was already becoming a household brand thanks to the success of Pyrex, and its executives were intrigued by the prospect of diversifying into the German-dominated Christmas market with war in Europe looming. Woolworth offered to place large orders for ornaments if they could figure out how to adapt their "ribbon machine," which Corning had been using to mass-produce light bulbs since 1926, to make the new glass baubles. Woolworth ordered more than 235,000 ornaments, and in December 1939 the first American-made glass ornaments were produced by Corning and sold in Woolworth's stores for a few cents each. In 1940, more than 45 million were sold. Corning also made "fancies," ornaments in the shapes of Santa Claus, elves, fruits, candy, and the like.

The ornament business was very good to Corning. A skilled German glassblower could produce about 600 ornaments per day; Corning was making several hundred thousand per day at its production plant in Wellsboro, Pennsylvania. Clear glass balls were shipped from Wellsboro to Max Eckardt's new decorating facility in New Jersey, where they would be hand-painted in luminous bright colors and boxed with the trade name Shiny Brite. They were silvered inside and out, with the promise that they would keep their "shiny, bright" glimmer for years to come, and remarkably, most of them have.

Print advertisement for Corning Christmas ornaments, 1940s.

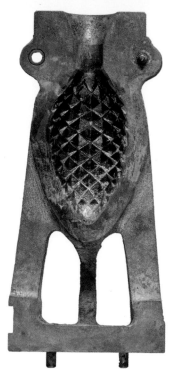

Two-part Christmas ornament molds, manufactured by
Corning Glass Works, Wellsboro, Pennsylvania, 1940–55.

Ornaments being decorated at the Corning Glassworks.

Striped-top Christmas
ornament manufactured
by Corning Glass Works,
ca. 1940s–60s.

Boxed set of Christmas ornaments manufactured by Corning Glass Works, 1950s.

Outdoor decorating kit manufactured by Corning Glass Works, 1967–73.

Graphic designer Robert Brownjohn (1925–1970) pushed the Christmas ball to its artistic limit when he created a wave-like holiday sculpture for the lobby of Pepsi-Cola's headquarters in New York City in 1958. The installation was composed of hundreds of Christmas balls in bright colors, arranged on a supporting structure that twisted and curled like a Möbius strip. Brownjohn was a founding member of the design firm now known as Chermayeff & Geismar & Haviv, and he was responsible for the iconic cover of the Rolling Stones' *Let it Bleed*, as well as the opening title sequences of the James Bond movies *Goldfinger* and *From Russia With Love*.

Robert Brownjohn, Pepsi-Cola Convention Christmas Lobby Sculpture, 1958–1959. Gift of Don Goeman.

Lighting

If silvery glass ornaments made Christmas trees sparkle and shine, it was in the electric string light that the modern holiday display truly met its match. The rather dangerous practice of using real wax candles to illuminate Christmas trees originated around the same time as the tradition of decorating trees with edible treats. Christmas lights, like electricity itself, took a few decades to become widespread, but by the 1920s, 85 percent of American homes were wired. According to Jeff Carter, a major collector of vintage Christmas lights, General Electric was an early leader in the field with its Mazda Lamps, along with NOMA, a company that was formed through the consolidation of fifteen smaller manufacturers across the country.

Advertisement for GE lamps, General Electric Company, 1947.

In 1927, GE introduced the C9 outdoor Christmas bulb. By 1933, the coloring process was improved to make the colors more durable in winter weather. Like silvered Christmas baubles, they were painted from the inside. In the mid-1930s, GE unveiled the C7 lamp, which solved one of the major problems that afflicted early string lights: if one bulb burned out, the rest did too. This selling point would be adopted by other makers through the 1960s. Like most other manufacturers, both GE and NOMA temporarily devoted much of their production capacity to the war effort in the first half of the 1940s. In 1946, NOMA introduced its newest innovation, which had been on hold since the early 1940s: the Bubble Lite. Like an early lava lamp, the Bubble Lite flickered through a tube of liquid. More than 150 million Bubble Lites had sold by 1950.

Sales flyer for GE Lighting,
General Electric Company, 1963.

Joyous Christmas lights, 1950s.

NOMA Christmas lights, late 1930s–early 1940s.

The 1950s and '60s were the golden age of corporate how-to manuals, idea "treasuries," and recipe booklets, which offered consumers glossy magazine–style inspiration for how to decorate and make merry at home. Resources like the *Popular Mechanics Christmas Handbook* from 1951 and Theodore Saros's *Christmas Lighting and Decorating* from 1954 both capitalized on this interest and gave serious lighting enthusiasts ideas to last a dozen holiday seasons. GE sponsored home-lighting contests and even provided guides for people who wanted to run their own competitions. All of this seemed to work, according to Carter: "In 1953 there were about 44 million households in the United States. In that year there were over 300 million Christmas lights sold—25 percent of them were used outdoors. Based on retail sales, decorative Christmas lighting was a $90 million industry."

Popular Mechanics Christmas Handbook, 1952.

GLAMOURIZE Your DINING TABLE

By Morris Tanenbaum

INDIRECT lighting reflected from the ceiling above your dining table adds sparkle to the formal dinner without the tiring glare of direct lighting or the shadowy uncertainty of candles. The diagram above shows the setup, the spotlight under the table being trained on a mirror attached to the ceiling. The light beam passes through a 2⅜-in. hole bored in a table leaf. The size of the mirror, which is centered over the table, should be one half that of the table top. Use a projector-type spot lamp of 100 to 150 watts and mount it below the table top in a porcelain socket attached to a bracket. Enclose the light in a metal housing provided with a series of holes or louvers for ventilation. The wooden table leaf adjacent to the hole is protected with asbestos, and a glass centerpiece can be used to conceal the lamp. By forming flanges at the top of the metal lamp house, you can fasten it in place with screws.

CHRISTMAS
LIGHTING
and
DECORATING

GENERAL  ELECTRIC

"GE Christmas Lighting and Decorating Guide," 1963.

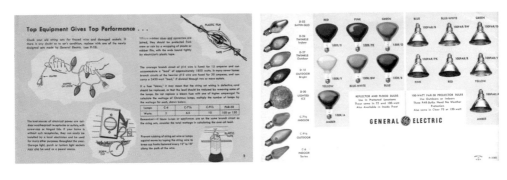

GE also had the ultimate showplace for demonstrating products and stylish lighting ideas: Nela Park in Cleveland, Ohio. Nela Park, the headquarters of GE Lighting, was first developed in 1911 by the National Electric Lamp Company (NELA) and later absorbed by GE. The 92-acre complex was the first modern industrial park in the world and was designed in neo-Georgian style to resemble a college campus. In 1933, it became the home of GE's Lighting & Electrical Institute, and it quickly became a kind of outdoor holiday lighting laboratory for the company, whose holiday displays remain a tourist attraction to this day. Each year, a miniature version of the National Christmas Tree in Washington, DC, designed by GE Lighting, is displayed at Nela Park.

Nela Park GE Lighting illuminated greeting cards, Cleveland, Ohio, 1958.

GOOD-WILL

Nela Park GE Lighting entrance decorated for Christmas,
Cleveland, Ohio, 1936.

Nela Park GE Lighting engineering building decorated for Christmas, Cleveland, Ohio, 1949.

Advertisement for Reynolds Metals aluminum trees and gifts, early 1960s.

BEAUTY AND CONVENIENCE YOU'LL ENJOY FOR MANY YEARS

Christmas Trees
and
Christmas Gifts
made with
Reynolds
Aluminum

HERE'S A "MERRY CHRISTMAS" combination for this year (and for many years to come) —a glittering, *permanent* Christmas tree of aluminum, with light, bright, and lasting aluminum housewares and utensils around it.

You'll use your new aluminum Christmas tree year after year, because it won't tarnish or shed; it's fire-resistant, completely clean . . . and it's so easy to set up, take down and store away. And the perfect gifts to go under these new aluminum trees are housewares and utensils made with aluminum.

They're light and easy to handle. They're strong, too—and won't rust or chip, ever. Aluminum housewares and utensils are "friendly" to foods—protect their true flavor. They spread heat rapidly and evenly for faster, easier cooking. And they're easy to clean and keep clean . . . remaining the perfect gifts for years to come.

Make this Christmas the brightest yet, with a tree and gifts made with sparkling, lasting Reynolds Aluminum. *Reynolds Metals Company, Richmond 18, Virginia.*

The Finest Products Made with Aluminum

are made with

REYNOLDS ALUMINUM

Aluminum Trees

One legend has it that the popular 1848 engraving of Queen Victoria and her family gathered around a decorated Tannenbaum popularized Christmas trees in America. Another one traces American Christmas trees back to the holiday customs of German Hessian soldiers who had settled in Pennsylvania in the eighteenth century and fought in the Revolutionary War. Historian Stephen Nissenbaum, author of *The Battle for Christmas*, suggests that both legends are a few decades off (the Hessians are too early, Queen Victoria is too late). While the custom certainly originates in Germany, it's more likely that the wholesale adoption of holiday trees in America was actually inspired by a nineteenth-century movement in German cities that was itself a kind of folk revival, rather than the uninterrupted practice of an ancient custom.

Like the nineteenth-century United States, Germany in the Victorian Age was rapidly industrializing and increasingly urban, with a growing middle class and a thriving consumer culture to go with it. Nissenbaum cites the popularity of various short stories that told of the (apocryphal) custom of German children preparing and decorating trees for their parents and siblings in an admirable act of industrious selflessness. The longing for a simpler and less commercial Christmas began to appear almost as soon as the holiday itself became commercialized. Nissenbaum cites an editorial called "Reflect Before you Buy!" that appeared in a New Hampshire newspaper in 1835, warning of the holiday's focus on gifts potentially inspiring materialism and selfishness in children.

This is precisely the message of the 1965 television special *A Charlie Brown Christmas*, which, in the wholesome tradition of the Grinch, sought to teach viewers, especially young ones, that presents and glittering holiday trappings were just the symbols that represented the real holiday miracle of love and friendship. The pink, cartoon metaphor for this duality is, naturally, an aluminum Christmas tree. Aluminum trees have an outsized cultural footprint in certain parts of the United States and even enjoyed a lovingly kitschy revival of sorts with the 2004 publication of *Season's Gleamings*, a book of photographs by the artists J. Lindemann and J. Shimon, who grew up in the aluminum-producing mecca of Manitowoc, Wisconsin.

A Charlie Brown Christmas, CBS Television animated special, based on the series *Peanuts* by Charles M. Schulz, 1965. Directed by Bill Melendez.

Aluminum Christmas trees were popular for a relatively short period, roughly 1955 through the mid-1960s, but during that time they came to symbolize the essence of postwar Christmas: they were lightweight, cheery, futuristic, and fun. It's telling that of all the different types of mass-produced holiday decorations that proliferated in the twentieth century—the shiny glass ornaments and the electric lights that replaced real candles, among others—aluminum Christmas trees had the shortest life span by far. Glass ornaments and string lights are as popular today as they ever were. So are artificial trees in general: today's synthetic evergreens, meant to look (and sometimes even smell) exactly like the real thing, easily deceive the eye of the most seasoned tree trimmer.

The Bob Newhart Show, "I'm Dreaming of a Slight Christmas." Featuring Bob Newhart as Bob Hartley and Marcia Wallace as Carol Kester Bondurant, November 7, 1973.

First made by Modern Coatings in Chicago, most aluminum trees—more than one million—were produced by the Aluminum Specialty Company in Manitowoc, Wisconsin, in the 1960s. Their most popular tree, the Evergleam, retailed for about $25. They varied in size, but generally took the same form: a wood or aluminum central pole would be drilled with holes at an angle, which would hold dozens of "branches," upon which strips of aluminum were twisted and fluffed to resemble the needles of an evergreen tree.

A miniature aluminum Christmas tree shown with vintage Shiny Brite ornaments, both ca. late 1950s to early 1960s.

An American Christmas card featuring an aluminum Christmas tree, 1960s.

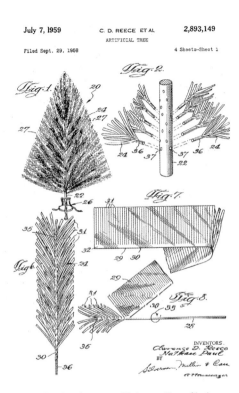

Patent for the Aluminum Christmas Tree, filed September 29, 1958, by Clarence D. Reece and Nathan Paul.

Because fingerprints would dull the shiny surface with oil, aluminum trees always looked best when brand-new and didn't age well. They also presented some decorating challenges: electric lights are not safe to use on their metal branches. But this limitation led to the development of the motorized color wheel, a rotating light that shone through multi-colored gels that would cast red, green, yellow, and blue light across the branches of an aluminum tree. Aluminum trees and assorted aluminum decorative products made it a point to advertise their use of Alcoa Aluminum, which, while not producing trees per se, offered advice in 1959 on how to decorate with aluminum as a DIY material and how to trim an aluminum tree.

Alcoa Aluminum newsletter, 1960.

HOW TO DECORATE YOUR NEW ALUMINUM CHRISTMAS TREE

"How to Decorate Your New Aluminum Christmas Tree," Alcoa Aluminum, 1959.

Proper decoration will make your aluminum tree more beautiful

Many thousands of American families now place Christmas gifts beneath a new type of Christmas tree—a tree made mostly of nontarnishing, long-lasting aluminum foil!

Foil trees are strikingly beautiful, with or without decorations. And with this beauty there is no fire hazard or dropping of needles.

The National Safety Council says any type of Christmas tree can be dangerous. The possibility of frayed light cords is a potential hazard whether the tree is a live green one, or made of metal.

This booklet, prepared by Aluminum Company of America, and reviewed by The National Safety Council for safety aspects, presents some ideas for decorating aluminum trees.

The decoration ideas come from the company's design consultant, Conny of Alcoa.

☆　　☆　　☆

Decorated with plain ornaments and inexpensive spotlights, aluminum trees develop a spectacular ethereal beauty. Each needle is a mirror-like strip of aluminum foil. The strips catch even the tiniest gleam of color or light, and reflect it with ice-clear brilliance.

The trees develop special beauty when illuminated by a colored spotlight—even without ornaments. Pink, green, blue, red, amber—any color or shade will do.

One spot is sufficient, although two will serve to heighten the outstanding effect.

Place the spotlight (or spotlights) in front or at the sides of the tree.

For more spectacular effects, a spotlight with a rotating color wheel can be purchased.* The rotating wheel slowly changes the sparkling color of the tree.

A rotating tree base is another "plus" that will heighten the brilliant appearance of an aluminum tree. As the tree rotates, it comes to life—looking like a beautiful metallic prism.

Remember: Use Underwriters' Laboratories approved electrical equipment!

Tip: When using a standard tree base, cover it with sparkling Alcoa Wrap household foil to match the tree.

☆ ☆ ☆

A spotlight, as the only decorating technique, produces a dazzling aluminum tree, especially at night. To add daytime color and brilliance, ornaments can be added. The mirror-like needles of the trees pick up the color of ornaments and reflect their color throughout the area surrounding each ornament.

Lovely effects can be achieved with ornaments of one color only, such as red, blue, pink or green. Ornaments can be the same size or, if you prefer, two sizes can be varied with excellent effect.

If ornaments of more than one color are used, they should be divided evenly as to the number of each color. Some unusually beautiful effects can be achieved with ornaments made at home. A series of designs and instructions, created by Conny of Alcoa, are presented later in this booklet.

Tip: Be certain to hang ornaments with wide hooks that will not distort the tree's foil needles.

With the use of spotlights, special tree bases and ornaments, aluminum trees reach the ultimate in beauty and safety. You may want to add your own touches, but stay close to the recommendations above to take full advantage of the inherent characteristics of the tree.

Some Do's and Don'ts

Before putting up your aluminum Christmas trees, check over this list of do's and don'ts to get maximum satisfaction from your purchase:

Do ... assemble the tree trunk first and place it in the stand.

Do ... when placing limbs into the trunk of your tree, start from the top down and place limbs carefully in holes in the trunk. Hold the limbs at the base, not in the center where you will bend the needles.

Do ... use spotlights to light your tree. Special effects include rotating color wheels or rotating tree holders.

Do ... decorate with glass or aluminum ornaments, preferably all the same color.

Do ... use wide-mouth ornament hooks.

Do ... when taking down your tree, remove ornaments carefully. Remove limbs from the top down, again holding them by the base near the trunk to protect the needles. Stored carefully in the original carton, your Alcoa aluminum tree will provide Christmas beauty in your home for years to come!

Do ... remember to use only Underwriters' Laboratories approved electrical equipment!

Don't ... tie on ornaments with string or wire that will distort needles. Use the wide-mouth hooks sold in all stores.

Don't ... put tinsel, chains or streamers around aluminum trees. They clutter the inherent beauty.

Don't ... display trees outdoors. Rain or snow can dull or stain the brilliant needles and destroy their beauty. If you want them seen outside, place them in a window or on a protected porch.

GIFTS & GREETINGS

Family lore holds that I figured out Santa's true identity sometime in the early 1980s because I was able to recognize my mother's distinctive cursive handwriting. At the time of the discovery, I vowed that if I were ever tasked with playing Santa one day, I'd learn calligraphy so that the thank-you note I left for the cookies and carrots would look appropriately antiquated. Even as a small child, I assumed that the old-fashioned, Victorian image of Santa Claus was who he really was. I had no idea that Santa had gone through a "Jetsons" phase.

Gene Kelly and Fred Astaire dance together on a Christmas-themed set with wrapped presents and stuffed animals during a photo shoot for *Life* magazine, 1958.

Midcentury modern Santa Claus cut a pretty sharp figure for someone whose primary means of transportation used to be a reindeer-drawn sleigh. In the nineteenth century, the idea that Santa was making toys by hand using old-fashioned tools added a nostalgic sheen to the business of holiday retail, disguising its coarser commercial side with a patina of wholesome craftsmanship. The postwar obsession with outer space, both as the site of scientific exploration and as the potential arena for a new kind of warfare, cast Santa's annual sleigh rides in a new light and made him an unlikely sci-fi character of sorts. Space was the place where Americans in the 1950s and '60s projected their highest hopes and their deepest anxieties. And because the night sky figures prominently in two major aspects of Christmas lore—the journey of the three wise men following the star of Bethlehem and Santa's global toy delivery—it made a certain kind of sense to weave it all together. It was probably comforting, too.

Christmas card,
"This Holiday Season,"
1957, USA.

This Holiday season...

Combat Operations Center at the North American Air Defense Command (NORAD), Colorado Springs, Colorado, 1950s.

The story of how the North American Aerospace Defense Command (NORAD) began "tracking" Santa's progress across the globe on Christmas Eve, 1955, seems too good to be true—and indeed it might be, but having been relayed in *The New York Times* and confirmed by NORAD itself, it could also be a genuine Christmas miracle. Legend has it that a child misdialed the number in a Sears® print ad for a Santa Claus hotline in Colorado Springs in late November and reached NORAD by accident (some versions of the story claim that the phone number in the ad was misprinted). The child allegedly reached the crew commander on duty, Colonel Harry Shoup, who was initially gruff with the caller. Shoup later came to see it as a public relations opportunity for NORAD (then called CONAD) when a member of his staff mounted a picture of Santa Claus on an aircraft tracking board as a joke. He then asked Colonel Barney Oldfield, public relations officer, to issue a press release that NORAD would "continue to track and guard Santa and his sleigh on his trip to and from the US against possible attack from those who do not believe in Christmas."

Santa's foray into the world of science fiction played out in movies, on TV, and in comic books throughout the 1950s and '60s. The camp classic *Santa Claus Conquers the Martians*, which promised a glimpse at a "fantastic Martian toy factory," took the story of sci-fi Santa to the next level by offering an account of what could have happened had his space travel finally led him to another planet.

Santa's Soviet counterpart, the white-bearded Grandfather Frost, called *Ded Moroz* in Russian, also took flight, and in holiday cards from the 1960s and '70s he was depicted monitoring the progress of the rockets and satellites from the Soviet space program. In the USSR, the holiday of New Year's was a secular version of Christmas, encouraged by the state as a kind of replacement holiday for Christmas and Hanukkah, both of which, like all religious observances, were outlawed. New Year's resembled Christmas in many ways, including the decoration of the New Year's tree, which looked for all the world like a Christmas tree with ornaments, surrounded by presents for good children delivered by Grandfather Frost on December 31.

New Year's card from the USSR, ca. 1960s–1970s.

С НОВЫМ ГОДОМ!

Greeting Cards

Midcentury Christmas cards featured a dizzying array of images, some of which were cozy evocations of an old-fashioned Victorian Christmas, while others radiated pure Atomic Age kitsch. And the creations of professional designers like Robert Brownjohn, Henry Dreyfuss, Charles and Ray Eames, and Theo Crosby took the path-breaking graphic sensibility of the postwar design world and fused it with the playful spirit of Christmas.

American Christmas card, gold stamp on paper, 1957.

The most widely recognized name in any kind of greeting card is Hallmark. Founded in 1910 by businessman Joyce Hall, who saw opportunity in the postcard craze of 1903 while working in his family's general store in Nebraska, Hallmark Cards remains the largest producer of greeting cards in the United States. Hallmark began selling Valentine's Day and Christmas cards under the name Hall Brothers, and during the 1920s and '30s they expanded to produce wrapping paper and cards for a wide array of holidays and occasions, adopting the name "Hallmark" in 1928.

Robert Brownjohn, Donna, Eliza, and Robert Christmas card, lithograph, late 1950s.

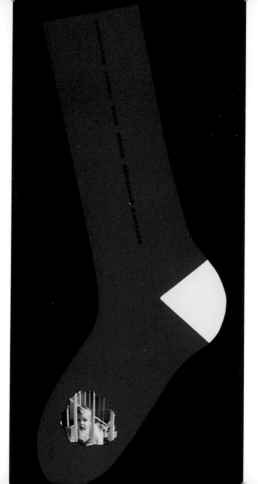

Leading figures in the postwar design world, for all their seriousness about modernism, sent each other cheery cards that would be a delight to find in the mail even now. Charles and Ray Eames were both copious letter writers, and their holiday cards often featured images of themselves in funny poses. A selection of their cards from the 1940s shows them variously reflected in a glass Christmas ball, floating inside a Christmas ball in miniature, and dangling ornaments against the backdrop of a modern sculpture. On the reverse sides, Ray's charming handwriting and drawings accompany the couple's greetings. Graphic designer Robert Brownjohn, whose Christmas ball sculpture adorned the lobby of Pepsi-Cola headquarters in 1958, created graphic Christmas cards both for his own family and for corporate clients. A stylized Christmas stocking features a circular photograph of his infant daughter Eliza from the late 1950s, and another from the same period designed for Masterset Brushes, Inc. shows the top of Santa's red cap peeking out of a white brick chimney.

Robert Brownjohn, Masterset Brushes, Inc. Christmas card, lithograph and cotton, late 1950s.

Henry Dreyfuss, whose iconic designs include the Hoover Model 65 convertible vacuum cleaner, the Westclox Big Ben alarm clock, and the Princess telephone, sent holiday cards to friends, notably Charles and Ray Eames. His 1945 card shows what appears to be a red-nosed reindeer, only to reveal when unfolded an extra-long dachshund with the word "greetings" written across his body. His tail supports a sign, tied with red ribbon, which reads: "From all the Dreyfusses." And interior designer William Pahlmann drew and collaged whimsical cards by hand, even dreaming up two "concept trees" in 1955 for the Fine Arts Group of Southern California Assistance League, which asked prominent designers to submit holiday decorating ideas for its annual fundraiser.

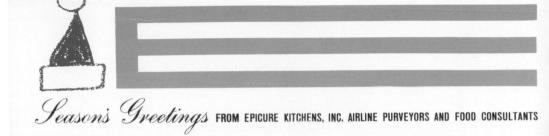

Robert Brownjohn, Epicure Kitchens Christmas card, lithograph, late 1950s.

Henry Dreyfuss, Christmas card from "all the Dreyfusses" to Charles and Ray Eames, ca. 1950s.

Christmas card (photograph) from Charles and Ray Eames showing Ray holding an ornament with an abstract sculpture behind herself and Charles, December 1942.

Christmas card (photograph) from Charles and Ray Eames showing them reflected in a mercury glass Christmas ornament, December 1941.

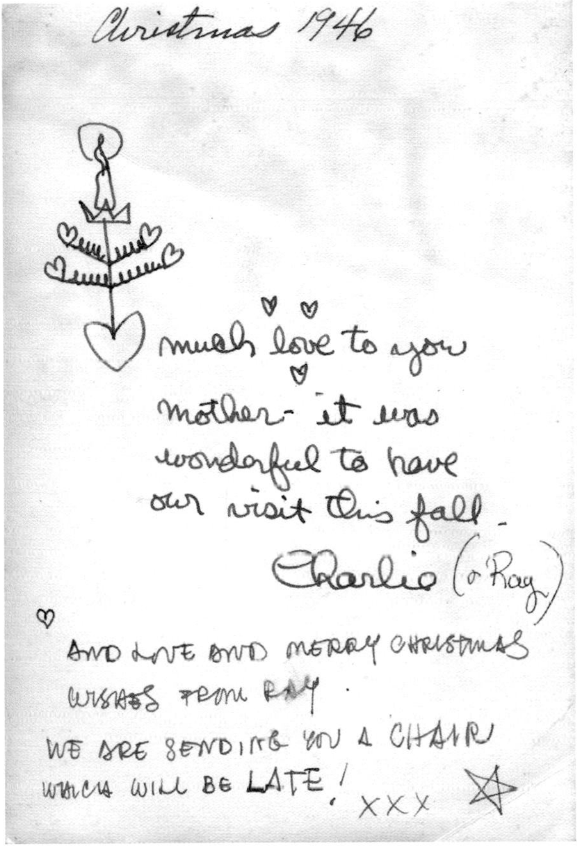

Christmas 1946

much love to you
mother- it was
wonderful to have
our visit this fall.
Charlie (+ Ray)

AND LOVE AND MERRY CHRISTMAS
WISHES FROM RAY.
WE ARE SENDING YOU A CHAIR
WHICH WILL BE LATE! XXX

OPPOSITE: Christmas card (photograph) from Charles and Ray Eames showing them waving from inside an ornament or snow globe, December 1946.

LEFT: The back of the card, with a drawing by Charles.

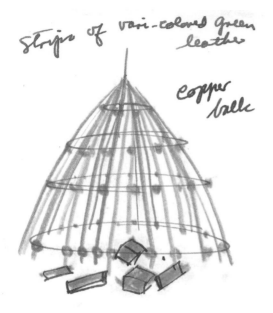

strips of vari-colored green leather

copper balls

leather Xmas Tree

inside completely filled
with copper wrapped packages.

William Pahlmann, leather
Christmas tree sketch for the
Christmas tree at the Fine Arts
Group of Southern California
Assistance League, 1955.

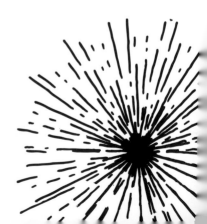

Greetings!

Bill Pahlmann

William Pahlmann
Christmas card, mid-1950s.

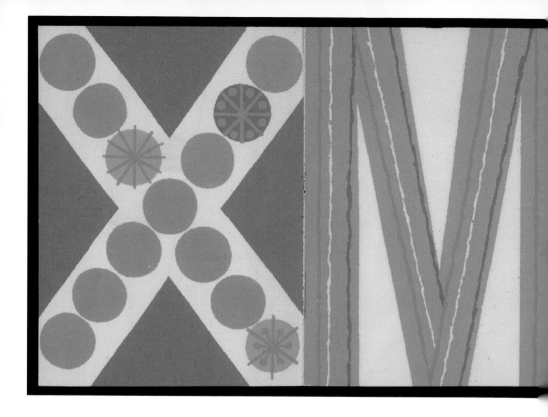

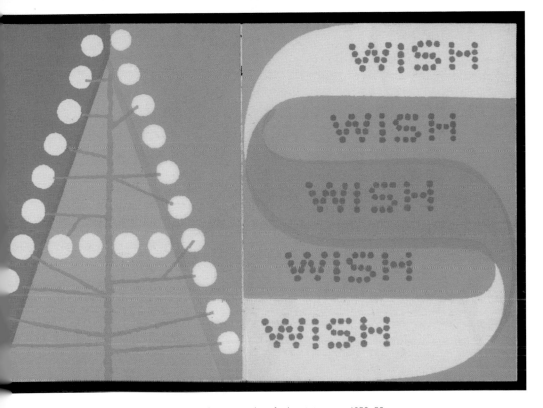

Frederick Hammersley Christmas card to an unidentified recipient, ca. 1952–53.

Space Age cards for the mass market, both from major producers like Hallmark and smaller companies that have since folded, featured a mixture of old-fashioned scenes and very of-the-moment depictions of a rocket-powered Santa or atomic-style trees and ornaments. One fold-out card from the early 1960s depicts Santa Claus flying a rocket loaded with toys and decorated with Christmas tree and snowflake stencils on the exterior. The card itself folds out into a paper template that can be cut and folded to create "your own spaceship," essentially a Santa Flier or fancy paper airplane. A similar card shows Santa with two elves, dressed in red suits and overalls, holding tools and pointing to a blueprint of a streamlined sleigh. Though their aprons and toolbox look quite old-fashioned, their pose echoes countless photographs of NASA engineers at work from the 1950s and '60s. And where Santa isn't present, trees and toys usually are. One especially vibrant card from the late 1950s shows three Christmas trees, two of which appear to be artificial—one flocked and one aluminum. All three have tree stands with tiny balls at the end of each leg, making them resemble a model of the atom. The ornaments are classic bauble shapes, with a few birds and bells, and the evergreen tree in the center has a Sputnik-style tree-topper.

American Christmas
card, 1950s.

Here comes Santa's **SPACE SHIP**
Full of cards and toys . . .

Zooming in to
wish for you
Lots of
CHRISTMAS JOYS!

How to make your
own SPACE SHIP:

Cut out ship and wing on heavy lines. Cut two slits as shown. Fold under on dotted lines. Then fold dotted lines in white triangles down and in, so that A is against A, B against B, and you have a solid red nose cone. Scotch tape space ship together at bottom front and rear. Insert wing tip D into slit D, fold down Santa and tuck him through rear slit. Attach two paper clips, one over the othe at bottom of nose cone. Use rubbe band on lower front notch to se space ship into orbit.

American Christmas card, 1960s.

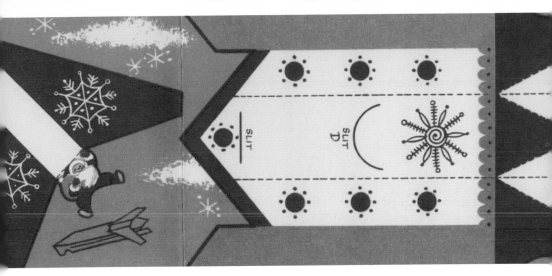

American Christmas
card, 1950s or 1960s.

Christmas Wishes

American Christmas cards, 1960s.

American Christmas card, 1960s.

TO WI

American Christmas card, 1950s.

A man loaded with gifts enters the subway at 34th Street, the stop nearest to Macy's department store in New York City, 1960.

Shopping

One of the most beloved Christmas movies of all time, Miracle on 34th Street, takes place in Santa's home away from the North Pole: an American department store. The plot of the movie is classically postwar American: its finale features the formation of a new family that moves into a large suburban house. Santa Claus is the character who helps make this happen, fulfilling the wish of Susan, the daughter of single mom and successful Macy's events director Doris Walker (Maureen O'Hara). Susan tells Kris Kringle, as he's referred to in the film, that she wants a real house, not just a doll's house. She doesn't want to live in a Manhattan apartment; she'd prefer a childhood in the country with a mom and a dad. And in the end she gets her wish, because her mother and their neighbor, Fred Gailey, fall in love. Kris Kringle is, of course, the real Santa Claus in the movie, with a real beard, and an uncanny command of any language spoken by a child waiting in line to see him.

The gag of the film, that Kris is the "real thing," demonstrates how pervasive department store Santas were and to what lengths stores would go to fashion magical settings for them in their toy departments. Marshall Field's in Chicago, Macy's in New York City, Wanamaker's in Philadelphia, and countless other stores across the United States created temporary "villages" with elves, sparkly decorations, music, and costumed staffers. Wanamaker's in Philadelphia was famous for its monorail, which circled the toy department on the eighth floor from 1946–84. Designers at Marshall Field's in the late 1940s created a display called the "Cozy Cloud Cottage," which resembled a modernist house in California or South Florida, complete with sliding screen doors, white brick, and a flat roof, all decked out with ribbon and ornaments.

Christmas display at Marshall Field & Company, Chicago, Illinois, 1956.

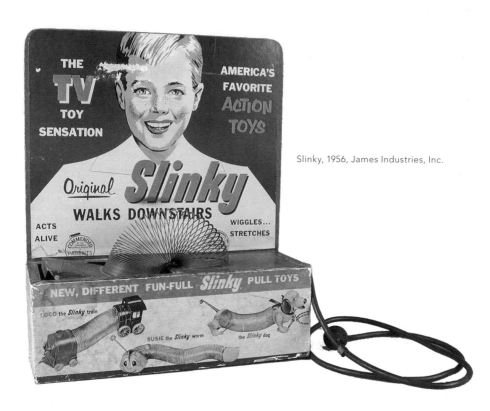

Slinky, 1956, James Industries, Inc.

Two employees of Pan American Airways in the toy department of Macy's department store in New York City at Christmas during their world trip, a journey of 26,000 miles in twenty-five days. *Picture Post*, December 1954.

STUFFED ANIMALS

Before the advent of online shopping, wistful Americans could "window-shop" at home thanks to magazines and catalogs. The Sears® Christmas "Wish Book," which first appeared in 1933, was a much anticipated visual feast of gifts and toys, almost encyclopedic in its scope. It was also an arbiter of style: the 1958 edition featured a close-up of a white-flocked artificial tree decorated with shiny, pastel-colored ornaments.

The Sears® Christmas "Wish Book," 1958.

SEARS
Christmas Book
1958

SHOP SEARS EASY TELEPHONE WAY
For numbers to call see pages 260 to 263
Index starts on Page 257   Easy Terms on Page 264

ORNAMENTS SHOWN ARE SOLD ON PAGE 336

SEARS, ROEBUCK AND CO., PHILADELPHIA 32, PA.

Gift-Wrapping MAGIC

Popular Mechanics Christmas Handbook, 1952.

I TS WHAT'S in the gift package that counts, to be sure, but there's no getting away from it—the wrapping creates the first impression. Nothing will take the edge off lively anticipation so much as a messy, hard-to-undo package.

The first step in thoughtful holiday gift wrapping lies in the correct selection of paper and ribbon. The size and shape of the package and the taste of the recipient should be carefully considered. Large patterns are available for large packages, small designs for the little parcels. Frequently a part of a large pattern is perfect for a spe-

cific small package. All that is required then is to center the paper properly on the face of the package so just the desired part of the design is highlighted. The bow should then be placed on the package so that it does not cover the design and ruin the desired effect. Diagonal patterns and stripes are especially good for round boxes. All-over repeat patterns allow for a bow almost anywhere, but pictorial designs should be left to show, with a bow off to one side. Appropriate designs in wrapping paper should be selected to suit the recipient's taste, whether it be masculine or feminine,

Wrapping Paper

The origin of the modern wrapping paper industry can be traced back to Hallmark. The Hall Brothers were enjoying an exceptionally busy Christmas season in December 1917 and ran out of their standard tissue paper, leaving them to use fancier printed paper as a temporary workaround. They sold it for ten cents per sheet. This turned out to be a huge hit with shoppers, who asked for it the following year. Midcentury wrapping paper tended to mimic the printed textiles of the era. Unlike cards, which feature one or two images, wrapping paper "repeats," like wallpaper or upholstery fabric, so small patterns that look good in multiples lend themselves well to wrapping paper designs. Recognizable images of Santa, holly, candles, or gifts were popular, as were Christmas balls and trees.

RIGHT: Wrapping paper, "Christmas Trees," ca. 1940–59, made by the Crystal Tissue Company. Print on paper.

OPPOSITE. Wrapping paper, "Star of Bethlehem," ca. 1940–59, USA. Print on paper.

American gift wrap, 1950s and 1960s.

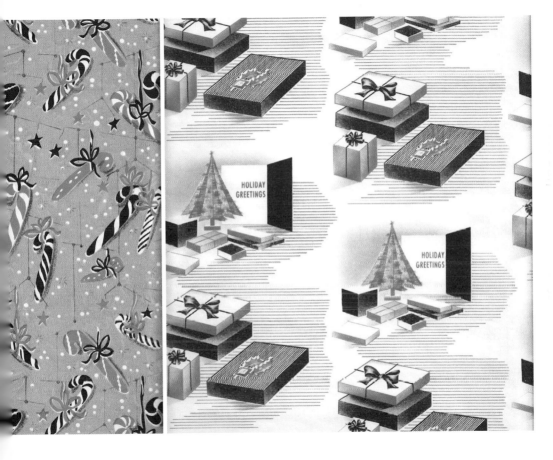

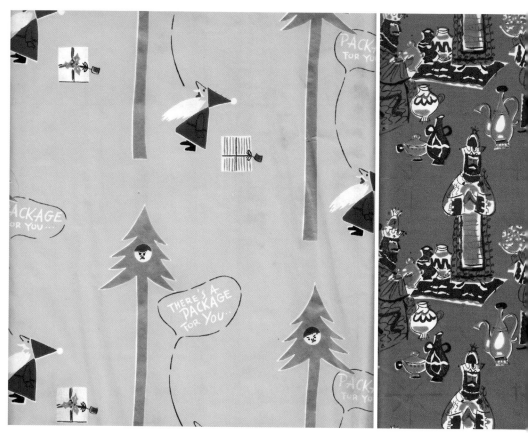

American gift wrap, 1950s and 1960s.

A young girl sits and speaks on a toy telephone, holding a Raggedy Ann doll near her play kitchen, 1955.

Toys

Toys in the postwar period were more colorful, dynamic, heavily marketed, and gender specific than ever before. Toys have long served as a kind of mirror version of the adult world, offering children a way to play at adulthood, trying out miniature versions of the everyday objects that form the adult world. Tiny stoves, domestic appliances, and tea sets; dolls, dollhouses, and doll clothes; chemistry and erector sets; little cars; telescopes, microscopes, and art supplies of all sorts let kids try certain aspects of adulthood on for size, and in the 1950s and '60s, if toys are any indication, the toy-making adults of the world focused their attentions on science, technology, domesticity, and fashion. The postwar period made playtime look like a pint-sized mock-up of House Beautiful crossed with Scientific American: little boys were encouraged to play scientist and engineer, and little girls were enticed by colorful working appliances or a chicly outfitted Barbie.

The Slinky was invented in 1943 by a naval engineer named Richard T. James and first demonstrated to the public at Gimbels Department Store in Philadelphia in 1945. James was stationed at a shipyard in Philadelphia during the war, and he was working on the development of springs that could be used to stabilize ships carrying sensitive equipment in choppy waters. Accidentally knocking a spring off his work table, he was intrigued to find that the spring appeared to "step" as though it was walking down a flight of stairs over a stack of books and onto the floor. He experimented with different sizes and shapes of steel wire, eventually fabricating a spring that could "walk," to the fascination of neighborhood children. James's wife, Betty, named the toy "Slinky," finding it in the dictionary and deciding that the word evoked the sound of the spring "walking." The first demonstration at Gimbels made use of an inclined plane. The following year, in 1946, the Slinky premiered at the American Toy Fair.

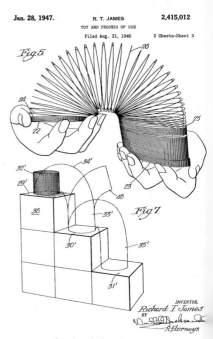

Patent for the Slinky,
filed January 28, 1947,
by Richard T. James,
James Industries,
Upper Darby, Pennsylvania.

A boy watches a demonstration of a Slinky "walking" down steps, 1946.

Kenner's EASY-BAKE OVEN

BAKES WITH 2 ORDINARY ELECTRIC LIGHT BULBS!

SAFETY FEATURES built in

COMPLETE WITH 3 SLIDE-THRU BAKING PANS, KITCHEN UTENSILS AND MIXES FOR BAKING EVERYTHING YOU SEE

Watch it bake

Enclosed Oven

Enclosed Cooling Chamber

KENNER'S EASY-BAKE OVEN

white cake mix

chocolate frosting

devil's food

Bake your cake and eat it too!

IT'S QUICK! IT'S EASY! Simply add water and bake these delicious treats: Devil's Food Cake, iced • White Cake, iced • Brownies • Vanilla Cookies • Biscuits • Apple Pie • Pretzels • Pizza • Candy. Baking times approximately 6 to 16 minutes.

"Cook Book" tells how to Easy Bake. You can get Kenner Refill Mixes or use Mom's ingredients.

EASY: While one pan bakes, another cools. Slide in 3rd pan which pushes others thru enclosed oven and cooling chamber.

HOW TO USE YOUR Kenner's EASY-POP CORN POPPER

pecan cookie mix

Just at the moment when real appliances were starting to appear in bright colors to coordinate with stylish American kitchens, the iconic Easy-Bake Oven appeared, offering little girls a taste of postwar domestic bliss. The first Easy-Bake was produced by Kenner in 1963, and in that year alone more than 500,000 were sold. Although contemporary versions of the Easy-Bake Oven are styled differently (they resemble microwave ovens today and are produced by Hasbro), the essential elements haven't changed: the oven is sold with packets of cake mix, round pans, and a light bulb that heats and bakes the miniature cakes. Easy-Bake Ovens originally had 100-watt bulbs as their heating elements and came in pale yellow or turquoise, mirroring the fashionable hues of the era. As the sixties progressed, the color palette changed, and by 1969 the "Premier" line of ovens came in avocado green and deep red.

Easy-Bake Oven,
Kenner Products Co., 1964.

My memories of Barbie are mostly concerned with her hair: at some point in the mid-1980s, I got my hands on a Conair hair crimper, which came with a zigzag crimping iron designed to emulate the most au courant hairstyles. I had more latitude to use the crimper on Barbie's hair than my own and, alas, it didn't fare too well. Still, Barbie was always chic and somehow seemed pulled together, even in nonstandard outfits or with experimental '80s hair. That's no accident: she was the first American doll specifically designed for kids to look like an adult.

When Barbie was first introduced in 1959 wearing a zebra-striped swimsuit, no one knew that she would amass a worldwide following, scores of outfits, a car, or a Dream House, but in retrospect, it seems inevitable. Barbie's creator, Ruth Handler, observed her daughter Barbara playing with paper dolls and noticed that she enjoyed giving them adult identities, yet most dolls during this period were modeled on babies and children, meant to be cared for rather than looked up to.

Barbie's Dream House, Mattel, Inc.,
Hawthorne, California, 1962–65.

The idea of a grown-up "role-model" doll was new, and Mattel executives were initially unimpressed by the idea. Handler created Barbie in 1956, using a German doll called Bild Lilli as a template. Bild Lilli was based on a newspaper comic character, and she was portrayed as a professional, beautiful woman who was independent and witty. Bild Lilli was originally marketed (oddly enough) to adults, but her array of fashionable outfits made her an instant and unexpected hit with kids, and herein lay Barbie's appeal some years later. Mattel would later buy the rights to Bild Lilli, which stopped production in 1964, and Barbie's empire went global. She was initially marketed as a "Teen-age Fashion Model" (the single word "teenage" was not yet common in popular speech). Around 350,000 Barbie dolls were sold during the first year of production. Barbie was one of the first toys in the world to benefit from extensive advertising on television, which has since become a de rigueur practice for the toy industry. Current estimates place the total number of Barbies sold worldwide at more than 1 billion in more than 150 countries.

The millionth Barbie sold in Germany, 1965.

Chemistry sets are among the oldest of "modern" toys, with their origins in the seventeenth- and eighteenth-century fascination with minerals and metals. Chemists, pharmacists, and medical students had portable chemistry sets that could be used in the field, and wealthy people (of both sexes) with an interest in science purchased elaborate kits of various types. Somewhere in between a toy and a hobby, such kits were the ancestors of the modern chemistry set, which, like toy microscopes and telescopes, was designed to inspire scientific curiosity in children—generally boys. The earliest commercial chemistry sets were manufactured in the United States mainly by the Porter Chemical Company under the "Chemcraft" trademark, and by the A. C. Gilbert Company, which introduced pink chemistry sets in the 1950s that encouraged girls to become "laboratory assistants" rather than chemists in their own right. Through the 1950s, sets like the Atomic Energy Lab included real radioactive ore, which was subsequently eliminated, along with some other chemicals, due to rising safety concerns in the 1960s.

Gilbert Chemistry Experiment Lab No. 12055, manufactured by A. C. Gilbert Company, New Haven, Connecticut, 1950s.

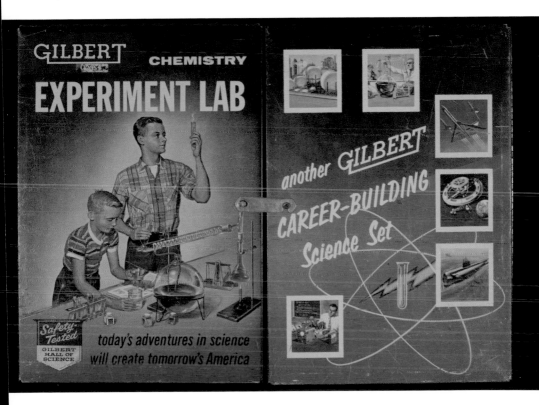

Chemcraft Chemistry Lab featuring Atomic Energy, manufactured by Porter Chemical Company, Hagerstown, Maryland, 1950s.

Well before the moon landing in 1969, the lure of outer space, strange planets, aliens, and futuristic ray guns captured the American imagination, and a whole new category of toys took flight. In the 1930s, science-fiction comic books and radio programs popularized characters like Buck Rogers and Flash Gordon, inspiring early "ray guns" like the Flash Gordon Radio Repeater (made from tin) and stylized action figures. After World War II, Japan began to produce robots, often with outer space or atomic themes, including Mr. Atomic. The *Tom Corbett, Space Cadet* TV series (popular in the 1950s), *Star Trek*, and, of course, NASA itself inspired the production of toy space capsules and rockets, made all the more exciting on July 21, 1969, when kids could watch as astronaut Neil Armstrong became the first human being to set foot on the moon.

Macy's department store featuring space toys on the shelves, New York, 1957.

Glenn Sitterly, four years old, demonstrates his space suit and disintegrator pistol on a rocket ship ride at the American Toy Fair, New York, 1953.

The New Yorker, "Space Toys for Christmas" cover illustration by Anatol Kovarsky, December 9, 1961.

In the upscale department store I. Magnin, guards keep a careful watch over a bejeweled Christmas tree as a well-dressed customer admires the $1.5 million worth of gems that decorate it. Los Angeles, California, December 1955.

Grown-Up Gifts

Before Christmas was rebranded as a family-friendly holiday that centered around children, gifts tended to run to adult tastes for things like books, clothes, fine food, jewelry, and other keepsakes. But postwar grown-ups got to play house just like their kids in the 1950s and '60s, when it seemed that everything from a new stove to a washer-dryer to a sleek, red typewriter—at least, as far as advertisers were concerned—was as exciting and fun as a new toy. Santa Claus himself, or more specifically his office workflow, advertised the new IBM Dictaphone in a 1966 print ad. "With this 28 ounce unit," Santa says, "I don't have to trust important things to memory, like who gets a football. And who gets a diamond necklace." IBM advertised its office machines more generally in a colorful ad featuring a mod, stylized tableau of gifts with the tagline: "Ever find IBM under your Christmas tree?"

Advertisement for IBM, 1966.

Gee, is it wrong to keep the gift you planned to give?

Not that I ever would, mind you.

Still, it's hard to part with a gift as practical as the new IBM 224 Dictating Unit.

With this 26-ounce unit, I don't have to trust important things to memory. Like who gets a football. And who gets a diamond necklace.

All I do is talk to it. Names and places and gift lists are recorded on magnetic belts. Quickly and smoothly. (Along with my famous collection of chimney dimensions.)

The IBM 224 is small enough to fit in a Christmas stocking. And so handy that it works anywhere. (From the North Pole to a chic Fifth Avenue shop to a lively toy department.)

Good grief, everyone gets a gift except me.

But maybe if I casually mention the IBM 224 to Mrs. Claus...

For shopping information on the New IBM 224 Dictating Unit, check the Yellow Pages under Dictation Equipment.

IBM®

ever find
IBM
under your
**Christmas
Tree?**

If you've ever wondered how the good things under your tree were made and delivered in time for a merry Christmas morning, the last thing you might think of is a battery of busy IBM machines.

But it's a fact: in thousands of bustling workshops and stores throughout the world, IBM data processing systems help in the manufacture and distribution of toys and clothes and all the other wonderful things that enter into your holiday giving.

Yes . . . every day, in uncounted ways, IBM helps add to the pleasure of daily living . . . speeds the progress that makes for many, many merry Christmases!

IBM | DATA PROCESSING

DATA PROCESSING
ELECTRIC TYPEWRITERS
MILITARY PRODUCTS
TIME EQUIPMENT

Advertisement
for IBM, 1960s.

Other companies relied on the lure of color to sell evergreen products like furniture and appliances. The General Telephone System told consumers to "Give Color" in a December 1957 print ad in which a bright red Model 500 Telephone, designed by Henry Dreyfuss, is held up as a perfect holiday gift. Cosco Metal Furniture presented an array of affordable card tables, playpens, serving carts, room dividers, and chairs, styled with holly and evergreen branches, and displayed by a model sporting a Mrs. Claus-style red dress with white fur trim. Santa Claus appeared to spring from a jack-in-the-box holding a blue Smith Corona typewriter in a colorful print ad from 1955. And for GE and Westinghouse, major manufacturers of appliances and kitchen gadgets, Santa was portrayed as the harbinger of domestic bliss. A print ad that appeared in *The Saturday Evening Post* in the late 1950s declared: "Santa Claus and Westinghouse are in cahoots!" and noted that their appliances, like automatic coffeemakers and pop-up toasters, "say 'Merry Christmas' 365 days a year."

Advertisement for Cosco Metal Furniture, 1958.

Christmas and Cosco go together!

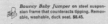
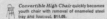
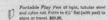
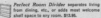
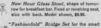
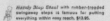
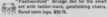
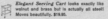

This new self-dialing phone is a wonderful convenience for people working without a secretary—the busy executive or housewife. Numbers frequently called are punched in code on plastic cards. With a card in the slot, you press the start bar and the number is dialed automatically. Card-Dialer phone, about $3.50 monthly plus installation charges; available from your local telephone company.

Gifts you couldn't give before

● Here are 16 of the most exciting gifts of the year. Why? Because most of them were still on the drawing board at this time last year, so very few people even know about them. Each is designed to perform a specific function useful in contemporary life. The prices range from a few pennies to hundreds of dollars, so your choice is wide. All are practical, useful gifts, perfect presentations for those on your list who seem to have everything.

The know-how of an expert carver is built into this electric knife. By merely pressing the control switch and guiding the knife, its reciprocating blades cut meat, uniform slices, thick

He will have the world at his fingertips with this small three-band portable radio. It receives international short wave, weather alerts, and marine broadcasts, as well as standard AM

ABOVE: *House Beautiful*, December 1963.

RIGHT: Advertisement for Olivetti, December 1957.

Now in handsome colors: the Olivetti Lettera 22, the portable portable. Traveling companion, family friend, student's delight, it provides all the important features of big standard typewriters. Blue, green or gray, $88 plus tax.

olivetti

The Olivetti Studio 44 is a somewhat larger portable, with the feel and features of a standard; type on it blindfolded and we think you'll mistake it for one. Blue or gray, $115 plus tax. Olivetti, 580 Fifth Avenue, New York 36, N. Y.

LIGHT,
BRIGHT,
LASTING

Christmas Trees
and
Christmas Gifts
of
Reynolds
Aluminum

Advertisement for Reynolds Metals foil gift wraps, 1960s.

Advertisement for General Telephone System, 1957.

Paul Rand illustration for El Producto Cigars, "Santa's Favorite Cigar,"
offset lithograph on paper, 1953–57.

Throughout the 1950s and '60s, GE advertised its array of products for both inside and outside the home, from portable hair dryers and television sets in fashionable colors to waffle irons and strings of electric lights for holiday decor. Though the company was strongly associated with particular kinds of goods, particularly light bulbs, GE made an effort in its advertising to promote the ideas of technology and newness as its own signature selling point, knowing that the gadgets of any particular holiday season would be nearly obsolete a few years later. In one double-page ad from the mid-1960s promoting portable TVs, the tagline read: "Progress is our most important product."

Advertisement for a
General Electric portable
television set, 1960s.

where a console will. Aluminized picture tube. Dark-contrast safety window. Terra Cotta with Ivory or solid Bermuda Bronze. 144 square inches of picture area. Model 17T026 shown.

3. Personal Portable—less than 13½ pounds … as little as $99.95.* Fits on a bedside table, yet brings in a clear, sharp picture. In Bermuda Brown or Peacock Blue—with Ivory. 43 square inches of picture area. Model 9T002 shown.

See them at your General Electric dealer's—while he still has some! General Electric Company, Television Receiver Department, Syracuse 8, New York.

Progress Is Our Most Important Product

 GENERAL **ELECTRIC**

*Manufacturer's suggested retail price which includes Federal excise tax, one-year warranty on picture tube, 90 days on parts. UHF at small additional cost. Prices subject to change without notice.

CHRISTMAS IS IN YOUR HANDS

Christmas and craft go hand in hand. Homemade and handmade are sometimes the ugly ducklings of Christmas gifts, but however they look, it's hard not to be moved that someone would spend the time and energy to create something unique for someone else, when simply buying something has never been easier.

House Beautiful, December 1963.

During World War II, Americans were encouraged—by the Office of War Information and, curiously, by corporations—to do without things, and to spend their money on war bonds instead of holiday gifts. Some companies capitalized on this by offering products in tandem with the purchase of war bonds. In the issue of *Life* magazine from June 11, 1944, an ad for The Hoover Company explained that the company was making war equipment instead of vacuum cleaners, and used its paid ad space to share tips on how readers could make their homes "war-shortening households" by conserving and reusing materials.

"Santa Claus Has Gone To War." Office for Emergency Management War Production Board, ca. 1942–43.

Magazines like *Woman's Day*, *Better Homes and Gardens*, and *House Beautiful* began publishing ideas for how to make holiday decorations and ornaments by hand, using non-rationed materials. Powdered Lux soap could be used to make convincing fake snow, and even natural objects like shells or pinecones could be fashioned into ornaments. After the war, companies that made materials that had previously been rationed, like Reynolds Metals (aluminum foil) or DuPont (cellophane), began advertising ways to use these new materials in DIY holiday decorating projects, and magazines followed suit, carrying on an inventive wartime tradition in the era of postwar abundance.

Advertisement for DuPont cellophane, 1949.

"SCOTCH" BRAND *Cellophane Tape leads to* *Christmas Magic*

*Fascinating peeking . . . the clever,
deceptively easy gift wraps possible when you
team everyday objects with "SCOTCH" BRAND
Cellophane Tape. It "sticks like crazy"!*

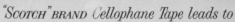

Your handiest Christmas helper. In 25¢ and 39¢ dispensers, 59¢ large economy-size roll.

© 1959 3M Co.

Front row, left to right:

GIFT WRAP GROOMING.
Package beauty begins when
"SCOTCH" Cellophane Tape holds
paper securely in place.

STAY-PRETTY WRAP. It still
looks pretty when box is opened.
Just cover lid and base separately.
Cut paper to cover lid, plus 1
inch extra on each side. Fold
edges inside lid and fasten with

tape (a). Cover base same as lid.
Idea shown: Arrange thin paper
strips in "x's" on table. Press
lengths of tape over "x's" to
pick them up and tape to box.

PICTURAMA. Child's play. Use
magazine scenes for gift paper.
For larger boxes, tape two or
more pictures together.

SPARKLING SYMMETRY.
Lovely! Wrap 3 loops of tape,
sticky side out, around a length
of cardboard; space evenly (b).
Place on box and press down
loops; slip out cardboard (c).
Repeat, alternating direction of
loops on package. Sprinkle with
glitter for the finishing touch.

Back row, left to right:

CHECKERBOARD. Imaginative!
Tape down equal-sized squares
of construction paper to gift
wrap. Make small loops of tape,
sticky side out (d) and place on
box. Press wrapped Christmas
candies to tape loops.

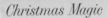

MONEY TREE. Attach new
pennies to gift wrap with tape
loops (d above) in rows as shown.
For extra glamor between pennies, fold back ends on lengths
of tape (e) and press, sticky side
out, to box. Sprinkle with glitter.

SNOWFLAKE DAZZLER. So
sparkly! Cut 2 snowflake shapes
from gift wrap paper. Use first
for package center; cut second
into four equal parts for corners
(f). Back up openings with cellophane tape and sprinkle with
glitter. Attach to box with tape
loops (d above).

We tend to think of the postwar boom years as a golden age for corporations, bolstered as they were by the dawn of television, supermarkets, and shopping malls. This was true, but it wasn't necessarily a dry spell for the homemade or the handcrafted, either. It was an early incarnation of the DIY movement, and it fused the ingenuity of wartime austerity with the material abundance of the 1950s and '60s. Food and craft project ideas were major features of magazine spreads, crystallizing the American homemaker's position as a domestic creative force whose raw materials were glossy and heavily advertised. Companies saw branding and sales opportunities in the rising popularity of DIY projects as hobbies for both kids and adults, and the world of Christmas crafting was an ideal platform to demonstrate a particular material's unexpected festive uses.

"Christmas Magic" gift-wrapping guide, Scotch Brand Tapes, 3M Company, ca. 1965

a hearthside supper for your tree-trimmers

By GRACE WHITE

IT's Christmas all through the house—garlands of greenery at the door, gala decor in every room, heavenly aromas in the kitchen. On these 10 pages we give you merry-Christmas ideas aplenty—with recipes and how-to instructions for all. Here, the fun of trimming the tree and a warming hearthside supper start the family's festive season

Recipes begin on page 64.
Instructions for making the decorations start on page 75

see buyer's guide

Santa's helpers ready to eat? Give them big mugfuls of hearty **Minute Minestrone** (a mix makes it speedy) with toasty buns; **Golden Oyster Scallop** decked with a parsley wreath; relishes; and the creamiest of holiday delights—**Eggnog Trifle**

Originally published in *Family Circle*® magazine, December 1958.

Do-It-Yourself, Inc.

The December 1958 issue of Family Circle *magazine contained how-to articles about making personalized felt stockings for each child in the family, as well as instructions for making "indestructible" Christmas ornaments out of paper doilies, pipe cleaners, glitter, glue, and ribbon, all products available at "variety stores." Amy Vanderbilt provided etiquette tips for how Christmas cards should be formatted, addressed, and printed (preferably signed by hand). A colorful spread picturing a family trimming their tree in front of an ultramodern white brick fireplace offered ideas for finger foods to serve during decorating parties, each image including a handcrafted piece of holiday decor alongside stylish displays of food and drink.*

The pages of *Better Homes and Gardens* were full of interior design ideas year-round and tended to focus more on interior glamour than family time. Nevertheless, the pages of *Better Homes* were full of festive ideas, including gifts for men that encouraged handyman tendencies, like power tools that could help outfit a "home workshop," though the tackling of actual needed repairs is rarely mentioned. An article called "Decorate with Nature's Gifts" in the December 1956 issue shows—at the height of the Cold War consumer boom—how families could create Nativity scenes, ornaments, and holiday decorations for their homes using everyday found objects like branches, dried seed pods, shells, and even live moss. The clear influence of folk art and the studio craft movement is evident in the images of project ideas like the "winter miniature," comprised of a piece of driftwood with evergreen branches, or the natural centerpiece that resembles a Japanese bonsai tree. And, perhaps knowingly referring back to the old practice of decorating with real fruit, this article suggests using shiny red apples and holly sprigs to welcome guests by the front door.

There's humble beauty in this nativity scene

Cornstalks, husks, and wheat straws are used with sticks and stones—and artistry—to build this charming nativity scene and Christmas creche.

For many centuries, the humble figures and familiar stable have been an important part of the Christmas decorations in homes around the world.

Here is one of simple beauty that you can make. It will be an absorbing family project. Detailed directions are given on page 155.

Start Christmas charm at your doorway with garlands of beauty and cheer

Photographs: de Gennaro, Hopkins, Weymouth

Decorate with *Nature's gifts*

By Fae Huttenlocher

You don't have to look very far to find lovely Christmas decorations for your home. And they won't cost much more than the price of your time and efforts.

Wherever you live—east, west, north, or south—there are natural materials all around you that lend themselves to handsome treatment. So, don your creative cap and take a look—to the fields and the forests and the seashores.

You'll note the subtle colorings of sun-dried pods, the graceful line of a barren branch, and the exquisite shapes of tiny shells. You'll find fruits, and nuts, and berries; weeds, and leaves, and mosses. Gather them in. These are the things that Christmas glory is made of.

To these basic gifts of Nature—yours for the seeing and using—add a few bright sequins and Christmas balls, a bit of ribbon and candle glow. With a deft hand, an eye for color, line, and proportion, you can fashion these simple materials into beautifully original, one-of-a-kind, and new-each-season arrangements.

Though you'll find yourself growing more self-sufficient with each new design, here are suggestions to start with.

More Christmas glamor for inside and outside the house ➡

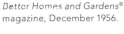

Decorate with Nature's gifts *continued*

Use Traditional Christmas materials, but give them a Contemporary flair

You'll enjoy this white "poinsettia" all winter. Paint magnolia or any large flat leaves and spray with canned snow while paint is wet. When dry, thread leaves at base on fine wire and coil around pinon cone. Touch top of cone with glue and glitter

Natural greens, cones, and gilded gourd "bells" make up this spirited centerpiece. Directions for bells are on page 155. For a really festive touch use red felt tablecloth and Noel candle Idorks. China is Ranier Pine pattern with Alpine tumblers

Much of the beauty of this handsome Della Robbia wreath—designed for a prominent red door— lies in the stunning color combinations. Cones, berries, and foliages are securely fastened to a firm background frame. Directions are on pa...

Photograph: Weymouth, Hopkins, de Genaro

Set the stage for the meeting of good friends. At your ho... open-house gatherings, use a lovely ensemble of natural g... The wall wreath, miniature pine-tree pillars in raffia wrapp... and a flat, narrow table swag give Christmas glamor to... cranberry punch served from a milk-glass bowl in matchin...

An espaliered Christmas tree studded with oranges and glitter... creates a striking effect in the Contemporary room. Apples, g... or any smooth, clean-lined fruit may be substituted to fit in...

..ast, West, and Southern Coasts you can
..lay shells that decorate these Christ-
..se you can buy them in interesting
..t at the dimestore. With tweezers, dip
..in cement or glue and then set in place

..se and seashells on a marine-blue cloth make a
..n and colorful setting for the Christmas Eve buf-
..Drape colored fish net at corner and mass glass
..nd Christmas balls on and around a bowl or tin
..with sand. Array table with bleached seashells

the bell at Christmastime

home and table decorations

fectly natural beauty

Use Nature's gifts from the sea to trim a lovely Christmas tree. The
shells of sea animals—some in their natural state, some painted, or
glittered and jeweled—make unusual and colorful decorations. You can
buy them at the market if you do not live where you can gather them

In the same issue, which contains print ads from both Reynolds Metals and Alcoa, advertising both aluminum kitchenware as holiday gifts and plain aluminum foil as a holiday decorating material, an article titled "Make these Dazzlers from Foil Plates" illustrates a project for kids using aluminum pie tins to create two- and three-dimensional displays. Pie tins can be stamped, crimped, painted, and decorated with glue and glitter to create unique Christmas ornaments and over-mantel displays, even shiny wreaths.

The December 1958 special issue, devoted entirely to holiday ideas, features elaborate decorating projects ranging from Japanese-inspired DIY Christmas trees to tropical-themed parties complete with colorful fishing nets and palm fronds. Another article in that issue on how to make trees from scratch dispenses with the idea of creating ornaments in favor of building a faux tree out of paper, foil, candy canes, and even yarn and cardboard, along with handcrafted paper cards and decorated gifts that look "too pretty to open."

... just no end to the decorative uses you'll find for foil plates. ...mantel ornament they're mounted in pine-tree shape. Cover ... circles with bright red cranberries and outline the tree with ...greens and cones. It will add brilliant *color* to your room and ...th radiance in the glow of candlelight. Directions page 165

Make this pretty tree with foil plate rims on a green metallic cone. Set a pair of them on the buffet or table for a glittering effect. Directions on page 165

...'re making your tree trims, cut 12 cute "stars" ...a plastic-foam wreath. Finish off at center with a ...te rim and 8 gold balls. ...g green leaves in a blue pillow vase are used here to ...interesting texture and color contrast to the hol-... decoration. Directions for wreath, page 165.

...t your tree sparkle in splendor with foil decorations. ...ey pick up and reflect the lights of the room and the ...w papers make them really glisten in color. ...Make the ornaments in graduated sizes, hanging largest ...n the lower limbs and smaller ones near the top. Your ...e will be more distinctive if one color dominates.

Originally published in *Better Homes and Gardens*® magazine, December 1956.

The 1959 *Alcoa's Book of Decorations* by Conny von Hagen is a treasury of design ideas that includes projects for Christmas, Easter, birthdays, and all sorts of other occasions. The Christmas section is the largest, and its subtitle says it all: "Christmas Is in Your Hands." Projects illustrated here include handmade baskets for stashing sweets created from the branches of a Christmas tree (echoing a very old European custom), foil stockings for the fireplace, foil accessories like Santa Claus's belt buckle and boots, foil angels (cone-shaped and relatively easy to make), and foil wreaths for the front door.

Instructions from *Alcoa's Book of Decorations* by Conny von Hagen, Golden Press, 1959.

PLEATING

BASIC METHODS FOR WORKING WITH FOIL

Aluminum foil makes it easy to create special decorations in your home. Here are some of the basic techniques devised for working with the versatile material:

PLEATING Accordion-pleated aluminum foil is needed for several of the designs in this book. It is simple to do and makes the foil stronger for forming large figures. To pleat, tear a sheet of foil of the desired length from the roll. Lay the sheet on a flat surface and fold over about an inch of the foil, beginning at one lengthwise edge of the foil. Now, double this folded portion back against the foil sheet, creasing foil to form another fold. Repeat this process, folding back and forth, until entire sheet is pleated.

CRUSHING Crushed foil can be used to make wreaths, letters, small animals, and many other ideas given in this book. Crushing is the basic operation for making the large animals in Conny's Zoo. Beginning with a sheet of foil, crush lightly with the hands along the lengthwise direction. This light crushing can result in circles of foil for various decorations, long ropes of foil, or narrow foil for forming letters.

COVERING Ordinary drinking straws covered with aluminum foil can make delightful mobiles and table decorations when combined with artificial flowers or nuts. A piece of aluminum foil about 2 inches long will cover a straw. Simply lay the foil on a flat surface, place straw on top of long edge, and roll straw, taking foil along with it. A group of these foil-covered straws, tied or wired together at the center, can be formed into a lovely starburst effect. Boxes of all types can be covered with aluminum foil. Cover top and bottom separately for smooth appearance and reusability of the gift container. Designs of colored tape, construction paper, poster paint can be used to "dress up" an ordinary box covered with foil.

MOLDING An almost unending number of shapes can be created by molding several layers of aluminum foil over an object of desired form. When removed, the foil retains the shape of the object. This technique will produce a bell by shaping Alcoa Wrap over a custard cup or bell-shaped glass. A reflector star can be molded using a common star-shaped candle holder.

FORMING CONE Cones are used in many of the designs in this book. They are easy to make and can be made of any desired size. Cut a circle of foil or paper and make a cut with scissors into the center. Now, form circle into a cone and hold with cellophane tape or glue.

CRUSHING

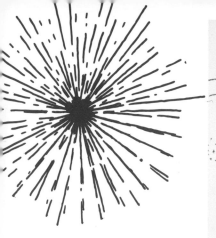

it's a container, a gift wrap, a centerpiece . . .
Just mold five Alcoa Wrap sheets over an inverted bowl. Cut off excess foil, leaving an even one-in. rim. Remove bowl. Repeat procedure to make top half; then crush a sheet of foil into a ball and place on top. Add two more foil sheets to hold head and top of body together. Remove bowl and cut rim. For the hat, cover a paper cup with felt, cut a brim. Use black buttons for coat and eyes, and a red one for the nose. The broom is a red paper fringe with a crushed foil stick.

cover photo—woven stars
Cut 2 in. strips of Alcoa Wrap, place straw on long edge and add a bit of white glue, then roll straw in foil. Cover four straws. Cross them in center. Hold straws and weave a ribbon in and out, as much as you like. Glue ribbon end to fasten. Cut straw ends to points and hang on a thin thread.

Instructions for crafting an aluminum snowman and table decorations, Alcoa Aluminum Newsletter, December 1967.

molded angel

To make this little angel your own, place a wad of foil on top of an inverted tumbler and crush three Alcoa Wrap sheets over it. Cut excess foil, leaving a narrow rim. Remove tumbler. For the face, cut a pink felt or paper circle, glue in place, then add eyelashes, a little red nose and a foil halo. Artificial flowers are pinned or glued around top half of face. The wings are cut from construction paper and taped to back.

mexican church

Use a medium size box. Cut away all but three sides. Mark and cut out towers, roof line and doors. Cover entire box with Alcoa Wrap. Cut out window frames, crosses, door and roof decorations from brightly colored paper and glue into place. Fasten small bells in each tower. Tape sides of box together to make a triangle. Fill with graceful candles and listen—you might hear the bells ring!

Better Homes and Gardens
TREASURY OF
CHRISTMAS
IDEAS

The *Better Homes and Gardens Treasury of Christmas Ideas*, a book published in 1966, contained scores of ideas with an even craftier bent, appearing as it did once the fiber art craze of the '60s and '70s was well underway. Ideas for festive wall hangings woven from yarn or made from felt feature bright colors and abstract designs, while Christmas card ideas feature the techniques of stitching and knotting alongside folding and cutting paper for graphic effect. A loom is suggested as an ideal gift for a teenage girl.

Originally published in the *Better Homes and Gardens Treasury of Christmas Ideas*, 1966.

To create chenille trifles for tree flocked white or green, mold 12-inch chenille stems to desired shape. Draw stems together where necessary; secure them with wire or another stem. Curl stem ends by twisting them around a pencil. Add beads, plastic foam balls, sequins, or glass baubles for finishing details.

Perky and gay tree decorations below are made by gluing yarn in four colors around a cardboard cylinder. Each stripe measures about 1 inch wide. Cotton fringe balls edge bottom. Yarn loop serves as hanger.

Easy-to-make baubles on the right hold tiny gifts, as well as grace the tree. To create them, machine-stitch or glue felt, velvet, or velveteen covers to fit over small boxes, cups, or cans. Leave a space open for inserting and removing gifts. Trim trinkets with bangles, buttons, ribbons, sequins, tinsel, and beads.

Diamond-shaped ornaments have plastic foam cones held together by florist picks. Ends of florist chenille insert into apexes of baubles. Gold braid is glued along lengths of cones, around apexes. Foil stars attach to ornaments which suspend from chenille hangers tipped in glue and inserted into the ornament tops. Tassels connected to strings of beads attach to bottoms.

Originally published in the *Better Homes and Gardens* Treasury of Christmas Ideas, 1966.

Triangle tree bagatelles can be finished in a variety of ways, but each begins with a four-inch equilateral triangle of colorful construction paper. Centers of triangle sides are marked and creased between as drawing below illustrates. Then four or five of these units are stapled together at crease lines to form three-dimensional stars. For a two-sided design, two stars are stapled together back-to-back, overlapping or alternating the points. For contrast, design can have colors alternate around the star or between the front and the back or two sides can be joined with seals.

Another variation of the basic fold is formed by leaving the points free after stapling four or five creased units together at the fold lines. This is accomplished by stapling the points together flat with adjoining unit, or by overlapping the points and stapling them together. Colors for these variations may be alternated for special interest and effect, too. For other variations, decorate the unit centers or points with seals, stars, and cutouts. Hang on the Christmas tree with fine nylon filament wire or thread.

Material for trims above

Colored gift-wrapping papers   Gold seals or decorative stickers   Staples and stapler   Glue   Gummed tape

Procedure

Paper Balls:
Cut 20 paper circles of uniform size. Make a cardboard equilateral triangle with its points just touching edges of circle. Place triangle on circle, fold and crease the three visible portions to form flanges. Staple together on the creases, five flanged triangles to form bottom of ball. Repeat to form top but before stapling last two circles fix a shallow paper cone with double-faced tape (cut halfway across paper circle; overlap slightly). Place inside top to close hole where five points meet.

Thread hanging wire, ribbon, or string through cone.
Cube in three colors:
Cut six five-inch squares, two of each color. (Called A, B, C.) Fold each point to the center, forming a smaller box with the creases. Lay the squares with four in a line and three at one end forming a T shape. Join at

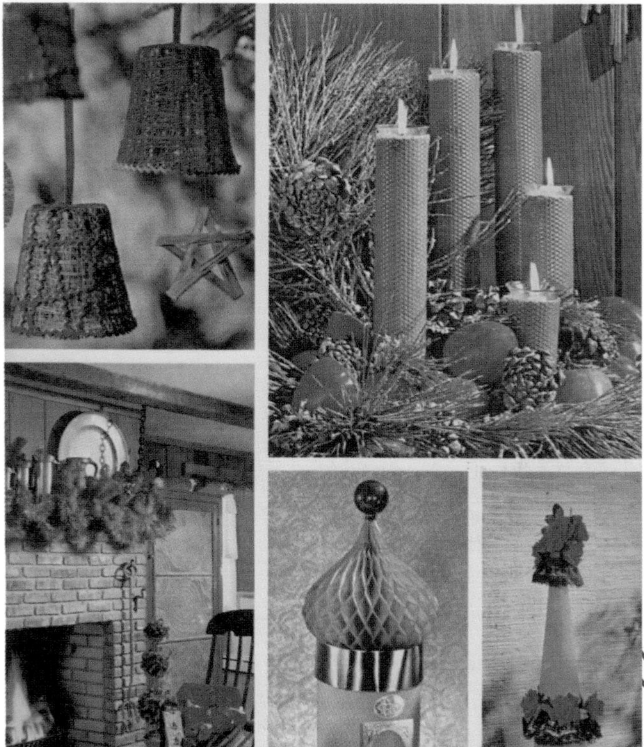

Originally published in the *Better Homes and Gardens Treasury of Christmas Ideas*, 1966.

Stoles above were knit on a hand made loom. Loom measures 33¾ x 27½ inches and stands 4¾ inches tall. An uneven number (45) of No. 16 wire brads are spaced ½ inch apart across the loom with ½ inch distance between parallel nails. Brads also extend ½ inch above surface of loom. To thread, use methods A or B below, running the yarn over every other nail one way, then back over empty ones. Repeat process so there are two threads around each nail.

To knit, take up bottom thread with crochet hook. Pull loop over thread above it, drop on other side of nail. Repeat step at each nail. Each nail now has one thread. Set up threading pattern again. Add one row

to get stacked effect. Knit off bottom threads as before. Continue until stole is as long as desired. Beginning on loom right, pick up end stitch on one rail, drop over corresponding nail on opposite rail. Take lower thread, lift over upper thread and nail as in knitting. Repeat for each pair of nails. Begin again at right, take loop off first nail, drop next. Knit off one thread. Take remaining loop off nail, drop over third nail. Continue to last stitch, fasten as in regular knitting.

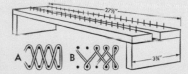

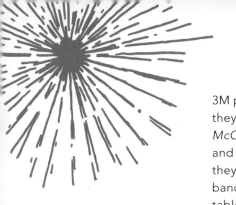

3M produced similar glossy guides in the late 1950s—they were circulated with issues of *American Home* and *McCall's* magazines. The 3M brands of Scotch tape and Sasheen ribbon are put to graphic use as though they were paints and brushes, with colorful stripes and bands running across walls, windows, presents, trees, tablescapes, cards, and of course, under the tree. An elegant DIY "stained-glass window" made with colorful cellophane and Scotch tape gives a modernist house with a big picture window a touch of faux-Gothic charm. Gifts are customized using tape to spell out names or "draw" the silhouette of a Christmas tree. Wreaths are fashioned from red ribbon, and fluffy white cakes are topped with ribbon flowers.

"Christmas Magic" gift-wrapping guide, Scotch Brand Tapes, 3M Company, ca. 1965.

CHRISTMAS MAGIC

FOR ALL YOUR GIFTS

USING "SCOTCH" BRAND TAPES AND "SASHEEN" BRAND RIBBON

A little bright tape and you're all set for guests!

*Get ready for compliments when "SCOTCH"
Brand Gift Tapes add holiday color to
centerpieces, place mats, windows . . .
your personal kind of "Christmas Magic!"*

1—Christmas Scroll. So pretty! Simply apply gift tapes—in decorative designs—to a solid color length of paper. Using "SCOTCH" Cellophane Tape, attach each end of paper to a rod (a). Suspend with wire.

2—Kiddie Cards. Children love making their own Christmas cards! All they need are scissors, paper and plenty of gay gift tape. *Note:* Do it yourself! Make family picture cards by framing snapshots with gift tape.

3—Your Own Motif. Napkin rings, place cards, match book covers, place mats, can all bear your own designs, initials, names. So colorful with "SCOTCH" Gift Tapes!

4—Gift "Frosting"! Make fruit cakes and cookies look even more tempting by decorating their Saran Wrap or cellophane coverings with holiday-bright tape. For "Stay Pretty" wrap shown here on cookie package, see last page.

5—Paper Figurine. Dramatic — easy! Simple cone shape topped with an ornament head. Held in place with cellophane tape, trimmed with gleaming gift tape.

6—Picture Window Tree. A charming way to greet your guests. Make a triangle pattern with newspaper. Trace it on your window with a crayon. Then apply gift tape along the crayon outline. For "diamond" effect, simply add parallel lengths of gift tape (b). Attach ornaments with matching gift tape. *Note:* Starbursts, candles, a church are other motifs to try.

Idea! Keep tape end handy! Hang rolls on edge of water glass.

"Christmas Magic" gift-wrapping guide, Scotch Brand Tapes, 3M Company, ca. 1965.

A potpourri of tips for home and gifts

◄ **WEATHERPROOF YOUR MAILING LABELS.** Smart and simple trick when mailing gifts. Protect addresses from ink-smearing snow or rain; cover them completely with "SCOTCH" Cellophane Tape to help assure safe arrivals.

◄ **GIFT TAGS.** A great new idea! "SCOTCH" BRAND Gift Tapes you can write on—plus bright stickers. 40 on a roll. Just snip them off and press down for new labeling speed and ease.

◄ **IDENTIFY GIFT GIVERS.** End "thank you" note mix-ups. Keep "SCOTCH" Cellophane Tape at hand during the bustle of opening gifts; use it to attach givers' names to packages (or to guess as they're opened).

◄ **STOCKING STUFFER.** Drop several rolls of "SCOTCH" Cellophane Tape . . . or left-over rolls of Gift Tape . . . in the youngsters' Christmas stockings. Just watch them put the tape to creative use during many play time hours.

◄ **DAZZLE WREATH.** Front-door dress-up with Glitter Bows (or any "SASHEEN" bow). Make "Magic Bows". Then press loop ends together (a) and cut V-notches in as many loops as you like. Back cutouts with "SCOTCH" Cellophane Tape and sprinkle with glitter. Form a wire coat hanger into a circle and tape or tie on bows.

◄ **CHRISTMAS STORY ON TAPE.** The holiday classic, "'Twas the Night Before Christmas", re-told and pictured on a roll of "SCOTCH" Gift Tape. Fun to tell from start to finish on children's gift wraps or Christmas cards.

◄ **CENTERPIECE CAKE.** Focal point of your festive holiday table . . . this gay cake with Fluffy White Frosting. Make 2 "Magic Bows" of "SASHEEN". Tie a bow to each side of a cluster of four candy canes; tuck in center of cake. Dot sides with crumbled candy cane.

COVER PACKAGES:

Front row, left to right: Tree Tapecraft, Gift tape makes tree design. *Glitter Magic.* Make Glitter Wanda (see "Friendship House" page). Fasten with a long loop of tape, sticky side out; press flat. Sprinkle with glitter. *Christmas Carnation.* Make "Magic Bow". Crush together loops, snip off ends (b). *Glitter Bow.* Make as in Dazzle Wreath, this page. *Name Dropper.* Spell out names with gay gift tape. *Back row, left to right: Bow Magic.* Make a large "Magic Bow". *Haram-Scarum.* Even left-over ends of gift tape look glamorous here. *Holly Bait.* Add sprigs of holly (or pine) using "SCOTCH" Cellophane Tape.

WRITE IN for the "how-to" of creating flower bows the "Magic Bow" way. From daisies to dahlias, these "SASHEEN" bows rate raves with little extra effort glamorize gifts. Send to Dept. GBC-129, 3M Co., St. Paul 6, Minnesota.

"SCOTCH", "SASHEEN", "DECORETTE" and "MAGIC BOW" are registered trademarks of 3M Co., St. Paul 6, Minn. Export: 99 Park Ave., N.Y. Canada: London, Ontario. "Magic Bow" and method of making patented U.S. Pat. No. 853835.

MINNESOTA **M**INING AND **M**ANUFACTURING **C**OMPANY

. . . WHERE RESEARCH IS THE KEY TO TOMORROW

3M COMPANY

IF THEY KEEP MOVING THE CHRISTMAS SEASON
UP EARLIER AND EARLIER, AN ADDED
FUNCTION OF THE HOME AIR-CONDITIONER
WILL BE KEEPING THE YULETIDE TREE
FRESH AND GREEN THROUGHOUT AUGUST
AND THE WARM EARLY SEPTEMBER WEEKS.

HOPE THIS BOOK OF CHRISTMAS QUIPS
HAS BROUGHT A SMILE OR TWO
AND THE HOLIDAYS WILL ALL ADD UP
TO HAPPY DAYS FOR YOU!

MERRY CHRISTMAS

AFTERWORD

A Charlie Brown Christmas *first aired on CBS on December 9, 1965, with its indelible, jazz-inflected piano soundtrack by Vince Guaraldi and perhaps the most famous aluminum Christmas tree of all time playing a starring role. In the five decades since, it's safe to say that aluminum trees have never quite returned to such prominence, but the postwar aesthetic and modernism itself have never been more popular.*

Hallmark Christmas card, 1960s.

Yet we don't know quite what to make of this time period; the cool chairs, Sputnik chandeliers, and graphic design we love today furnished a society that didn't give women or Americans of color their full civil rights. It gave rise to both the space race and the arms race. What *A Charlie Brown Christmas* captures so beautifully, and perhaps why it's still so well-loved, is that our feelings about shopping, feasting, decorating, and, indeed, Christmas itself are complicated, and always (at least since about 1830) reflect our fraught relationship with consumer culture. That Charlie Brown chose a beat-up, sad-looking little tree at the height of American Cold War prosperity—and that we cheer his good taste—speaks to the DIY, inventive crafter in all of us.

That spirit shaped the look and feel of midcentury Christmas in all kinds of ways that make perfect sense given the holiday's long history as a time of year for trying new things and cultivating a sense of wonder for young and old. Some chose to do so by harnessing the abundance and new materials of the era, while others dusted off their wartime grit by making their own festive fun with simple materials. Still others, like Theodor Geisel (aka Dr. Seuss) and Charles Schulz (creator of Peanuts), created lovable characters who ask us to take a good look at the miracles of love and friendship that surround us all the time, and celebrate that on Christmas, tree or no tree.

Popular Mechanics Christmas Handbook, 1952.

Building Blocks

Something new in building toys combines cardboard with grooved blocks. The blocks—some are cut at an angle—can be produced on a power saw

1½" OR LONGER
CARDBOARD
⅞" SQUARE
SAW SLOTS
45°

Pixy Banks

⅞" STOCK
COIN SLOT
CARDBOARD ARMS
¼" DOWEL
7" MAILING TUBE
SCREW
½" X 2" DISK
1½" X 4" DISK
TACK

Sections of mailing tube form the bodies of these little pixy banks, which can be made short or tall. Scraps of pine will do for the wooden parts. The squared drawing gives two different head patterns.

½" SQS.

½" X 5½" X 5½"

RUBBER-HEAD TACK
1½" X 1½" X 20"
½" X 4½" X 5½"
2½"
¾" X 1" X 7½"
¾" X 4" DOWEL

Doll Seesaw

Here's a simple toy that little tots can operate to give dolly a seesaw ride. The chair for the doll can be made to suit and the rest of the parts proportioned accordingly. Metal shelf brackets pivot the bar at the balancing point

CHRISTMAS CANDLESTICKS

HEAD 1⅝" DIAMETER
FLESH COLOR
⅞" HOLE
½" D.
⅛" D.
⅝" D.
⅜" D.
WING ⅛" STOCK
1¾" D.
1¾"
1½" D.
2⅛"
CANDLE HOLDER
1½"
2½" D.
6½"
1½" D.
ARM (SPLIT TURNING)
1" D.
SAW AND GLUE
1" SQUARES
2½" D.
SAND FLAT
CROWN
SAW GROOVE
3½" D.

COLORS
DRESS – LT. BLUE
HAIR – BLACK
CROWN – RED
CANDLE HOLDER – RED
WINGS – WHITE

WHITE
1¾
⅞" HOLE
1" X 4½"
1" X 3½"
1" X 2½"
RED
4¾"
BASE ¾" X 4" X 14"
1" D. X 4" DOWEL
BROWN
3½" D.
2" O.
BLACK
RED
FLESH
RED LINES
⅝" STOCK
1" SQUARES
WHITE
RED
RED SHOES
2¾" X 6½"

116

Give Santa a Hand

Route those toy orders to Santa through your workshop. Here are 10 wooden ones to bring shrieks of delight from your youngsters on Christmas morn

By Marvin Hartley

SANTA'S job will be easier when you turn toymaker and lend a helping hand to relieve the burden on his North Pole workshop. Among this group of 10 exciting toys, there's at least one that will surely make Christmas extra merry for some youngster. Except for the lighthouse stool, bucking bronco and the burp gun, which require some sheet metal, all of the toys are made mostly of wood. The step stool, shoeshine kit and novelty lamp can be made of scraps from your wood box. Construction of these, as well as the others, is apparent from the drawings, which include patterns for the parts that require jigsawing. Enlarging the patterns full size is easy. First, count the number of squares given and rule on paper an equal number of 1-in. squares.

30

Merry Christmas

MAKE YOUR OWN GREETING CARDS

By Paul Will

WHEN CHRISTMAS draws near, many take care of the greeting-card problem by simply going out and buying them. But the card that bears a really personal and sincere greeting is one that represents the handiwork of the sender. Today, most of the personalized cards are limited to the photographic type, largely because they can be mass-produced with a minimum of effort. While photo cards offer a variation from commercial cards, in most cases they lack color. However, there are several other types of greeting cards that can be duplicated in quantity, as well as color, on a production

Today, in the era of the Buy Nothing Christmas, our purchases are linked to something that Cold War Americans didn't worry much about: our carbon footprint. We talk now about focusing on experiences rather than things. And, in a sense, we have the postwar era to thank for this point of view, although all the shiny lights and new appliances might distract us. If there was one thing Americans knew how to do well in the 1950s and '60s, it was nesting and making the most of being at home. Sure, it didn't hurt that teenagers had their own Princess telephones and younger siblings could watch *Bonanza* on TV, all without leaving the house. But the focus on domestic life, playing games, baking, entertaining, decorating the tree, and undertaking perhaps ill-advised but nevertheless fun craft projects is exactly the kind of family-focused Christmas that the early Victorians imagined when austere St. Nicholas underwent his transformation into jolly Santa Claus.

Popular Mechanics Christmas Handbook, 1952.

At one poignant moment in *A Charlie Brown Christmas*, a forlorn Charlie Brown asks Linus what Christmas is all about, and—totally without irony—Linus recites the text of the Annunciation to the Shepherds from Luke 2:8–14. The last line is: "Glory to God in the highest, and on Earth peace, and goodwill toward men," which, according to Linus, is what Christmas is all about. Cold War Americans knew a thing or two about the wish for peace on Earth; after surviving two world wars and an economic depression, faced with the threat of yet another (far scarier) war with nuclear potential, their response was to cherish those close to home. Since the days before Yule and Saturnalia evolved into Christmas as we know it, the holidays of midwinter have been about enjoying time together and celebrating a job well done, whether it's final exams, the end of harvest season, or wrapping up a big project at the office. The look of the more commercial side of the postwar era may be a bit shiny and glossy for our artisanal tastes nowadays, but the inventiveness and creativity with which they celebrated together is still inspiring.

If you tire of shopping, and the spirit of the Buy Nothing movement inspires you, skip Black Friday, and take a cue from the craft experts of the 1950s to festoon your home with DIY holiday splendor. Or, better yet, pack up your supplies and spend time helping someone else who needs a dose of holiday cheer and some good, crafty company. Linus, Charlie Brown, and even Lucy would agree: that is what Christmas is all about.

A Charlie Brown Christmas, CBS Television animated special, based on the series *Peanuts* by Charles M. Schulz, 1965. Directed by Bill Melendez.

CREDITS